The House of Jastrzebski

The Extraordinary and Notable History
of an
Ancient Polish Clan

Compiled by

Marjorie Jaski, Esq.

The House of Jastrzebski: The Extraordinary and Notable History of an Ancient Polish Clan.

Copyright ©2025 Marjorie Jaski
All rights reserved. Attribution credits and references provided as applicable by law.

ISBN: 979-8-218-77798-2

(paperback-60 pages)
Cover and page design by Marjorie Jaski.
Cover Jastrzębiec Coat of Arms from Poland Archives.

Many thanks to KDP publishing services for their assistance in the preparation of this publication.

Printed in the United States of America

From Gniezno to NATO: Compilation Resources

This colorful journey through the history of Poland, as seen and lived by the Jastrzębiec Clan, has been compiled for those seeking a working knowledge of Poland's history. It is for educational purposes, generally, and not just for those commonly sharing the Coat of Arms. Because this clan appears within the first generation of establishing the Kingdom of Poland, it is representative of the length and breadth Poland has experienced as a country, and offers a unique vantage point of the extraordinary and notable developments of Poland itself.

Extensive resources were researched and incorporated into the preparation of this compilation. Authoritative excerpts and references for further reading have been included to guide the reader interested in further detail of an active history, with historic tales beginning in the 10th century. With appreciation and acknowledgement, some of the key resources contributing to this compilation include:

Arthive.com	Polish National Alliance
Britannica	Polish at Heart
Culture PL	Polska.fm
European Amino Blog	Pressmania PL
Geology.com	Radio Free Europe/Radio Liberty
Historia Poszukaj/Portal of the National Institute of Museums	Researchgate.net
Institute of National Remembrance	San Jose State University
International Encyclopedia of the First World War	Serve to Lead Foundation
Jaski, Jaster, and Serek family archives	Slavorum.org
Jastrzębska Spółka Węglowa SA (JSWA)	Southtown Economist
Jastrzebski Wegiel (volleybox.net)	Spokesman-Review
Life Magazine (archives)	Swarthmore Global Nonviolent Database
LRE Foundation (Liberation Route Europe)	The Atlantic Magazine
Maplogs.com	The Bastion Institute
Medievalheritage.eu	TheCollector.com
Medievalists.net	The George Washington Presidential Library at Mt. Vernon
National Archives	The Guardian News & Media
National Museum in Krakow	The Woodland Trust
National WWII Museum	Time Magazine (archives)
Osprey Publishing	Topwar.com
Outrider Stories	University of Virginia/UVA Today
Polish American Society of Charleston	U.S. Naturalization Records
Polish Culture NYC	U.S. Holocaust Memorial Museum/Holocaust Encyclopedia
Polish Genealogical Society of America	Warsaw Institute
Polish Museum of America	Wikimedia/Wikipedia/Wikipedia Commons
Polish Origins Forum	Yad Vashem/World Holocaust Remembrance Center
Polish Roots® (Polishroots.com)	Yankeedoodlespies.blogspot.com
Polish Greatness Blog (Awesome, Inc.)	

About the Compiler

Granddaughter of Jan and Eva Jastrzebski, Marjorie Jaski was born and raised in the city of Chicago where the family settled. After Graduating from Smith College, she earned advanced degrees in Community Health Sciences and Law, and has written and published several research compilations in other areas of review. She currently practices law and is a lifelong advocate of public health. Her professional biography can be found in "Who's Who in America".

About the History of Poland

The history of Poland spans over a thousand years, from medieval tribes, Christianization and monarchy; through Poland's Golden Age, expansionism and becoming one of the largest European powers; to its collapse and partitions, two world wars, communism, and the restoration of democracy. (Summary from Wikipedia, accessed 08/07/2025.)

> *The name Polans comes from the Proto-Slavic word 'pole', which means 'field' or 'open space'*

About the Coat of Arms in Poland and the Jastrzebiec Clan

Due to the antiquity of the clan, there are many Polish surnames originally derived from Jastrzębiec having little if any resemblance to the Jastrzab root name. An inspection of one's Coat of Arms, if known, is a reliable method to determine a clan relationship to this clan or any other Polish clan. For the Jastrzębiec Clan, the appearance of a horseshoe in the Coat of Arms is a unique and helpful indicator. The Polish Genealogical Society of America is an excellent source for further information in this area.

Table of Contents

About the Compiler iv
About the Coat of Arms in Poland and the Jastrzebiec Clan iv
Epigraph vi
From the Compiler vii
Notable Achievements Jastrzebski History Part I 1
On the Map: The Christening of Civitas Schinesghe 966 2
Jastrzebczyk from Early Medieval Period 3
Jastrzębiec Voivodeship: Poland's Leaders 4
Jastrzębiec during the Piast Dynasty 5
Jastrzębiec of the Late Middle Ages 7
Land Areas Developed by Jastrzębiec 9
Lex Zborowski EVOLVING POWER STRUCTURE IN THE 16TH CENTURY 11
Szlachta During the Polish-Lithuanian Commonwealth 13
Notable Acheivements Jastrzebski History Part II 15
Great Warriors: The Polish Winged Hussars 15
The Last Great Victory Defending the Commonwealth 1794 23
Three Partitions of Poland 1795 24
Related Families with the Jastrzebiec Coat of Arms 25
The Resurrection of Poland 1918 27
Notable Achievements Jastrzebski History Part III 28
Great Polish Warriors of the 20th Century 27
Victory in WWI Restoring Poland's National Sovereignty 1918 29
The Jastrząb and the Last of Partitioned Poland 30
The American Jastrzebski Clan Chicago 31
WWII Begins in Poland 1939 32
Warsaw Uprising 33
V-E Day Victory in WWII 1945 34
Roll of Honor Jastrzebski 35
The First Generation in Chicago 36
Jastrzebski Honored as Rescuers of Jews during WWII in 1962 37
The Jastrzeb Agreement 1980 37
The Second Coming of Poland 1981-1989 39
The "Free White Eagle" 41
The House of Jastrzebski The Next Generation 42
The Story of the Harvest Moon Ball Dance Championship 43
Chicago Southtown Economist March 2003 44
Jaster Golden Wedding Anniversary 2003 45
In Loving Memory 46
Other Notable Achievements from Jastrzebski(s) 47
Poland as Member of NATO 48
Appendix A: The Jastrzebski Clan Crest/Coat of Arms 49
Appendix B: The Legend of Lech and the White Eagle 51

Epigraph

From Poland with Love

Polishness is not just a matter of being born Polish.

Polishness is a choice of the heart, love of language, culture, history, pride in the achievements of past generations. Loyalty and adherence to the values enshrined in national tradition. Poles as a nation were formed with the Latin civilization adopting the motto God-Honor-Ojeczyna. The foundation of this civilization is Catholic ethics, and this means that being a Pole one must meet high moral standards.

Polishness is demanding, being a Pole is not easy. One must fulfill one's duties to the Fatherland and Compatriots, including at the risk of one's own life. At a time when one convinces oneself that one should live lightly easily and pleasantly, it is difficult to be a Pole.

-Gilbert Keith Chesterton
Epigraph from a Polish citizen and resident of Poland, 2024

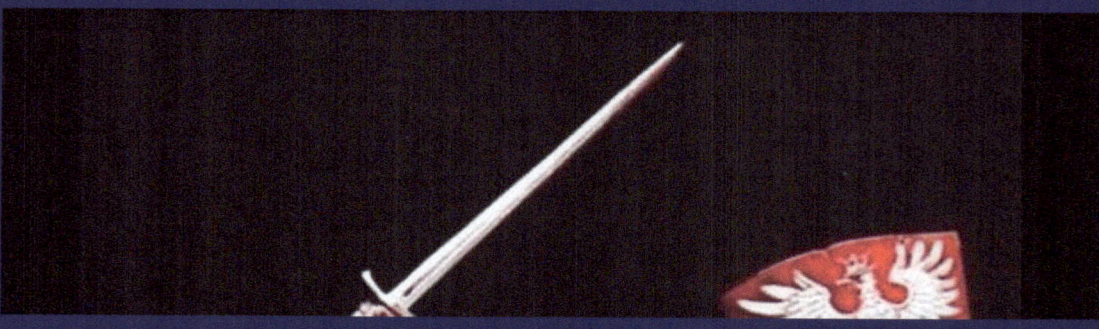

From the Compiler

I was in Washington, DC when I discovered my Polish ancestors were commemorated as **'Rescuers'** in WWII. Visiting the U.S. Holocaust Museum, I was surprised to learn of their recognition. It piqued my interest to explore the history of my Polish ancestors and contemporaries of Polish **grandfather Jan Jastrzebski**, who immigrated to Chicago in 1920. I soon discovered the ancient and current **Jastrzębiec Coat of Arms (COA)** and the extraordinary story behind it. Key excerpts of the story have been reproduced in the **Appendix** (p 49).

Jan Jastrzebski in 1920

The Jastrzębiec Clan, pronounced **'ya-shem-bee-ets'**, developed along with Poland itself, as they were among the original leaders of Poland from ancient medieval times. Both the name and the clan became well-established in land areas that even exist today. As surnames developed, Clan names evolved from 'Jastrzębiec' into '**Jastrzebski**' (**'ya-shem-ski'**, or in English **'ja-strebz-ski'**) and other Jastrzab derivatives. As documented in the 19th century, from the Jastrzebiec Clan sprung many additional surnames, seemingly unrelated to the Jastrzab original name (meaning *goshawk*), and yet still associated by the distinctive Coat of Arms. The 19th century list has been reproduced in **Related Families with the Jastrzębiec Coat of Arms** (p 25).

The Coat of Arms (COA) in Poland is the key to identifying those with a relationship to the parent clan— having a common ancestry or part of the Duchy or estates of a clan. '**Jastrzebski**' is but one form of the surnames associated with the Jastrzębiec COA, but is still the most recognizable tie to the original clan name. The consistent and unique trait of the Jastrzębiec COA is **the horseshoe** and (usually) **the goshawk.** Notably, Grandfather Jan kept the surname 'Jastrzebski' after coming to the U.S. as well as his American-born children. His two American-born sons would later 'Americanize' their surnames in post-war adulthood, as many did.

This overview of the Jastrzębiec Clan, from its origin to the present day, contains three sections each displaying extraordinary and notable achievements of the Clan and Poland, generally. The Jastrzębiec Clan was among the first recognized noble clans of Poland; male members were primarily military leaders (or part of their army), and later, also administrative or clerical leaders. The Polish cavalry during the Polish-Lithuanian Commonwealth of the 16th through 18th centuries were renowned throughout Europe, known as the **Winged Hussars**. They remained essentially undefeated for 200 years, significantly comprised of noble *szlachta*, of which the Jastrzębiec Clan was a part.

Jastrzebiec coat-of-arms signet-ring. This signet ring belonged to Czesław Jankowski h. Jastrzębiec. Hand made in 1943, with silver from an old Polish coin, by a prisoner at a Nazi-German prisoner-of-war camp for Polish officers.

The House of Jastrzebski (referring to the Clan as a whole) thrived through the Polish-Lithuanian Commonwealth, and was not disrupted even **through WWI.** Many served as military officers ending the partitioning of Poland that began at the end of the Commonwealth, **including Grandfather Jan**, age 22 when the war was over in 1918, allegedly having served as the General's valet during the war.

Yet unimaginable terror and destruction awaited Poland in **WWII**--in Stalin's **Katyn Massacre of 1940**, the **Warsaw Uprising of 1944**, and the notoriously widespread **German Nazi prison camps**. Today, the Polish clans of antiquity are still recognized and honored in Poland as the so-called "**Ancient Princely Houses**." Amazingly, other Jastrzebski descendants still exist. Grandfather Jan Jastrzebski was among them in his youth. Like many other Poles in 1920, he immigrated to **Chicago's Polish Downtown**. My father, Ernest Jaski, said his father's voyage was given as a courtesy of the Polish General, likely Gen. Jozef Pilsudski himself.

Jastrzębiec

Jastrzębiec is one of the most ancient Polish coat of arms. Dating back to the 10th century, it has been used by Poland's oldest szlachta families — Poland's Immemorial nobility — and remains in use today.

Notable Achievements

Jastrzebski History Part I

Early Medieval Period to the Commonwealth:

Tenth to the Late 16th century

On the Map:
The Christening of Civitas Schinesghe 966

With the christening of its first ruler, Mieszko, Poland symbolically entered into the orbit of Western civilization, and its name appeared for the first time in the annals of Medieval historians. 966 is precisely the moment when the historical memory of Poles starts. Other, earlier records of Poland belong to the domain of unverifiable fantasy - like the mythical father of all Poles, Lech; King Popiel (who was eaten by mice); or Piast, the founder of the dynasty that bred Mieszko.

Poland was known as "Gniezno state" or "Mieszko's state" until the name "Poland" was adopted soon after the conversion of the Polan territory to Christianity in 966.

Who was Mieszko?

Likely born in the 920s, Mieszko was born to Siemomysł, a ruler of the Piast dynasty, a family belonging to the local Slavic tribe of Polans, with Gniezno in Wielkopolska as their possible family seat. In the course of the late 9th and 10th centuries, the family was able to subjugate the majority of the Wielkopolska (Greater Poland) region. Historians connect these early military successes of the Piast dynasty with the new concept of his military retinue, a quasi-army called *drużyna*, whose soldier members were paid regular wages (rather than sharing war booty).

Civitas Schinesghe, also known as the Duchy of Poland or the Principality of Poland, is the historiographical name given to a polity in Central Europe, which existed during the medieval period and was the predecessor state of the Kingdom of Poland.
Wikipedia ›

Mieszko citations from **Shpakovsky, Vyacheslav** (16 June 2019). *Polish chivalry. From Boleslav the Brave to Vladislav Jagiellon*, Military Reviews. Topwar.com.
https://en.topwar.ru/158872- polskoe-rycarstvo-ot-boleslava-hrabrogo-i-do-vladislava-jagellona.html>; accessed 12/05/2024.

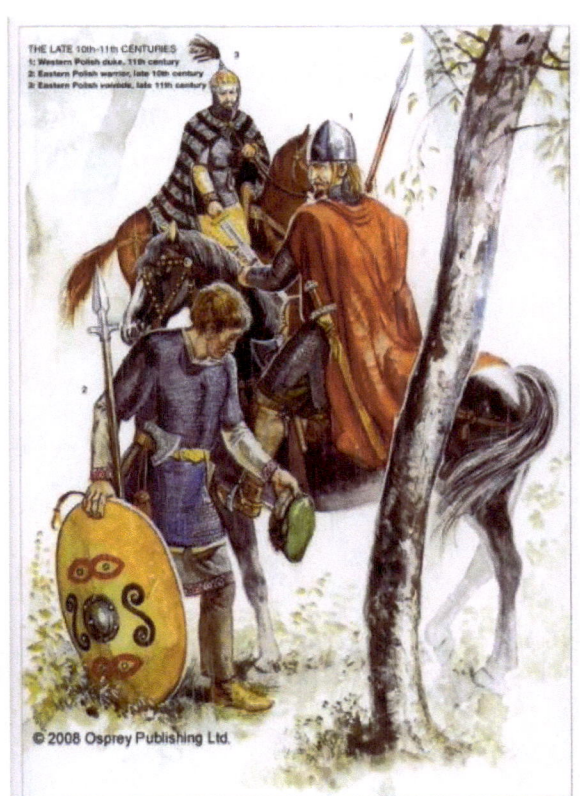

Polish duke, warrior, and voivode (*wojewoda*, originally meaning a warlord) from 10th and 11th centuries.

Source: David Nicolle, Witold Sarnecki "Medieval Polish Armies 966–1500", 2008, illustrated by Gerry Embleton and Sam Embleton / © Osprey Publishing Ltd.

Jastrzebczyk from Early Medieval Period

Writing in the 16th century, Polish-Czech writer and heraldist **Bartosz Paprocki** states this coat of arms is called Jastrzebiec because the clan's pagan ancestors bore a **Goshawk**, or **Jastrzab**. The antiquity of the Jastrzebiec coat-of-arms is also evident by the fact that no other coats of arms is borne by more families, including Paprocki himself. Paprocki says, in O herbach, that several hundred years ago the clan called themselves simply Jastrzebczyks. Not until after the days of **Archbishop Wojciech of Gniezno** did foremost members of this house began to write z Rytwian ("from Rytwiany"). Other members similarly named themselves after the estates they possessed.

Ancestors of this House: Voivodes and Bishops

Ancestors of this House

- Called Jastrzebczyks in 999
- Recruited by Duke Boleslaw the Brave (Mieszko's son; 1st King of Poland in 1025)
- The Holy See elevates Gniezno to an archbishopric in 1000

According to Paprocki, based on a named grant of privilege to a monastery, the most ancient member of this house was **Mszczuj**, Sandomierz castellan in 999 at the time of Boleslaw the Brave; his **two sons Mszczuj and Jan** signed their names as "from Jakuszewice" when made Krakow canons by Bishop Lambert in 1061.

Above right: East-West Schism of 1054 divides the Christian Church into Eastern Orthodox and Western Catholic Churches. Below: English translation of the 19th century heraldic reference *Herbarz Polski* by Kasper Niesiecki, excerpts from Polishroots.org/Research/Heraldry/HerbJastrzebiec?PageId=176; accessed 07/28/2025.

Silesian Bishop Jan of Wrocław was the first Pole to ascend the episcopacy. Bishop Jan of Wrocław, elected in 1062, presided for 10 years, and died in 1072. This is attested to by Dlugosz in Kronika, wherein he wrote that Bishop Jan of Wrocław was of the Jastrzebiec clan.

Paprocki cites a monastery grant of privilege given in 1199 for **Borzywoj and Derszlaw Jastrzebczyk, heirs to Jakuszowice**. He also includes **Piotr, son of Wojciech, the Sandomierz standard-bearer**. **Swentoslaw**, a pastor from Poznań and Gniezno canon, was chosen to be bishop of Poznań; already of an advanced age, he had retired, but he yielded to those urging him and accepted the office. He spent only a year at this see before his death in 1176 and was buried in the church. Paprocki writes that in Jędrzejów a grave from the year 1206 is covered with a stone on which the Jastrzębiec arms are still visible, but the letters can no longer be read.

Piotr Brevis (called Maly ("small"), as brevis is Latin for "short") was chosen to be the **nineteenth bishop of Plock** in 1254. In the fifth year of his episcopate, he moved to another see. However in Vitae Episc. Plocens, Lubienski ascribed no coat-of-arms to him yet wrote Piotr Brevis was of a noble clan. Paprocki in O herbach, added that Piotr Brevis was a Jastrzebczyk.

Additional forebears of this clan are **Michal, castellan of Kraków** in 1225; **Mistuj, voivode of Kraków** in 1242; **Scibor, voivode of Leczyca** in 1242; and **Msciug, voivode of Sandomierz** in 1342. A letter of Kazimierz the Great, King of Poland, given to the Strzelno monastery, mentions, inter praesentes, **Mszczuj, Kraków chamberlain**.

Jastrzębiec Voivodeship: Poland's Leaders

The origins of voivodeships go a long way back in history. They first appeared after a period of feudal division in the early Middle Ages. Infighting caused Poland to temporarily split into about a dozen principalities, and after it reunited these former divisions' borders were reflected in the shapes of the new regions of military governance now known as voivodeships. These military roots are even encoded into the Polish name for them: *województwa* (vou-yeah-voo-tz-tfah) which comes from the phrase *wodzić woje*, meaning 'to lead warriors.' The name points to the fact that the head of a voivodeship or a *wojewoda* was obliged to command its warriors in times of need.

Excerpt from Niesielski, Kasper as cited in <culture.pl/en/article/all-over-the-map-a-quick-tour-of-polands-voivodeships>. © 2019 Marek Kepa. Culture.PL publisher, updated 2022. Jastrzebczyk is among the original principality voivodes.

Excerpt below from Wikipedia, *Voivodeship*; accessed 09/25/2024.

Title of nobility and provincial governorship

Main article: Voivodeship

The transition of the voivode from military leader to a high ranking civic role in territorial administration (Local government) occurred in most Slavic-speaking countries and in the Balkans during the Late Middle Ages. They included Bulgaria, Bohemia, Moldavia and Poland. Moreover, in the Czech lands, but also in the Balkans, it was an aristocratic title corresponding to *dux*, Duke or Prince.

Jastrzębiec Castle

In 1425–1436, Bishop Jastrzębiec built a defensive Gothic castle in Rytwiany, surrounded by the swamps of the Czarna River. The castle, partly destroyed in 1657, was inhabited until the 19th century, then fell into a ruin, to be finally demolished in 1859. All that now remains of it is a fortified tower. In the early 17th century, when the village and the castle belonged to the family, it was a cultural center of the region. In 1621, Camaldolese monks settled (t)here, at the request of Jan Tęczyński, building an abbey and a church. The monks moved to Warsaw in 1819, and their church now serves as a local parish church. In the late 19th century, the Radziwiłł family owned the village and built a palace there.

Excerpt above from <en.wikipedia.org/wiki/Rytwiany>; accessed 11/24/2024.

Jastrzębiec during the Piast Dynasty

Wroclaw Cathedral, Wrocław, Poland - SpottingHistory

South-West Poland

Wroclaw

The bishop of Wrocław from 1062 to 1072 was **Jan** of Nysa, of the Jastrzebiec Clan, the first Polish bishop to hold this office after a period when only Italians had served. He presided over the diocese for about a decade, succeeding Hieronymus and being followed by Piotr I. His tenure coincided with a period of hardship for the diocese, which had been ravaged by a pagan uprising and was in a precarious state.

Bishop and Cathedral of Wroclaw 1062
Excerpt translated from Encyklopedia Wrocławia, Wrocław 2000

Krakow

More from the Jastrzębiec Clan in Krakow, Leczyca, Sandomierz, and Plock

Additional forebears of this clan are Michal, castellan of Kraków in 1225; Mistuj, voivode of Kraków in 1242; Scibor, voivode of Leczyca in 1242; and Msciug, voivode of Sandomierz in 1342.
A letter of Kazimierz the Great, King of Poland, given to the Strzelno monastery, mentions, *inter praesentes*, Mszczuj, Kraków chamberlain.

First mentioned in 1097, Sandomierz gained early importance because of its geographic position astride the trade route between the Baltic and Black seas and Ruthenia. It was the 12th-century capital of the Sandomierz principality and received municipal rights in 1286. Devastated by Tatar invasions in the late 13th century, the town was rebuilt in the 14th century by the Polish king Casimir III (the Great). Sandomierz developed economically and became one of the largest towns in Poland in the 16th century, but in the 17th century it was ruined by plague, fires, and prolonged wars. It passed to Austria in 1772 and was returned to Poland in 1918.

The Polish church rose during the Piast Dynasty (10th – 14th century). When the Piast dynasty came to a close in 1370, the bishops of Kraków provided spiritual and ecclesiastical leadership. They wanted to create a reciprocal relationship between the laity and the church. They were primarily interested in a stable dynasty under Kazimierz II Sprawiedliwy ('The Just'). Kazimierz helped increased Kraków's spiritual status when he aided Bishop Gedko in expanding the cult of St. Florian and had the Bishop translate the saint's remains to Kraków. Another Bishop, Iwo Odrowąż, pushed for the canonization of St. Stanislaw; who was officially canonized in 1253. Indulgences were granted to those who visited his relics and a Feast day was granted in the Polish monastic calendar in his name.

Krakow vs. Wroclaw

Krakowian ecclesiastics were interested in local ecclesiastical advances and stable, hereditary ducal leadership. They sought to liberate Kraków from secular dependence. Kraków competed against other cities like Wrocław for ecclesiastical distinction. Wrocławian Bishops had the same pretensions as Krakowian Bishops, and Wrocław was the stronger diocese but Kraków was historically lucky. The two cities struggled with each other for half a century. The Bishops of Kraków proved to be instrumental in bringing about Kraków's ecclesiastical prominence during the 13th century.

Piotr Brevis 19th Bishop of Plock 1254

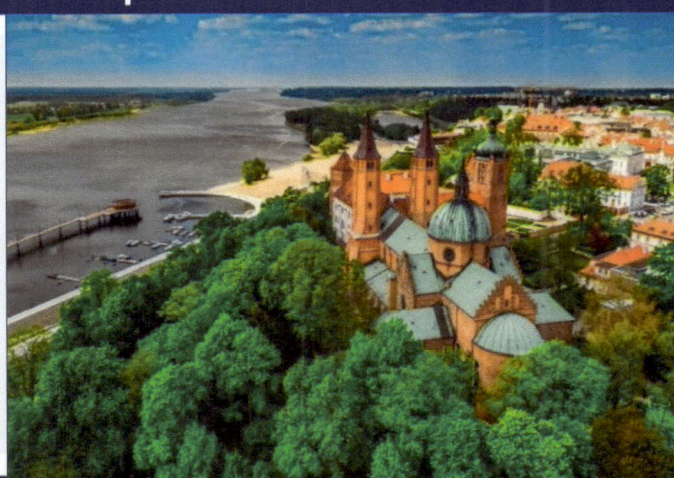

REFERENCES:
1. Krakow ecclesiastics cited from: Medievalists.net ©2024.<https://medievalists.net/2010/05/the-spiritual-authority-and-ideological-conservatism-of-the-bishops-of-krakow-in-post-gregorian-little-poland>; accessed 12/16/2024.
2. Plock photo from Pleven Municipality website: <https://pleven.bg/en/international-cooperation/plock-poland>
3. Bishop Brevis allegedly was called 'Brevis' because he was short.

Jastrzębiec of the Late Middle Ages

Andrzej Jastrzębiec (died 1398), also known as **Andrzej Wasilko** or **Andrzej Polak**, was a Polish Catholic priest and diplomat, a first bishop of Seret and of Vilnius. He was part of the Jastrzebiec ancestral line of the szlachta (noble families) of Poland. He joined the Franciscans and quickly rose through the ranks of the order.

The first verified mention of Andrzej Jastrzębiec dates back to 1354, when he was listed among the parochs in Mazovia. After a brief time spent as a missionary in the pagan Grand Duchy of Lithuania, he moved to the royal court of Hungary, where he became the confessor to Elizabeth of Poland, Queen of Hungary. From there he set off to Moldavia, where he spent several years as a missionary. As an effect of his mission, on 31 July 1370 a new bishopric of Seret was created and the following year Andrzej became its first bishop.

Władysław II Jagiełło, Duke of Lithuania became King of Poland after marriage to Queen Jadwiga in 1386.

Diplomat and Bishop Andrzej Jastrzębiec from the 14th Century (d. 1398)

Archbishop Wojciech Jastrzębiec of Gniezno
(Pontificate service 1423-1436)

Wojciech, became a priest, from being a Kraków scholastic, a Kraków dean, and Poznan pastor. He became the mitered prelate of Poznan in 1399. Tearing down the wooden church in Bensowa, he had a brick one built in 1407, and later settled the friars of St. Paul the Hermit there, and gave to it the villages of Bensowa, Bensowka, Bydlowa, and Bystronowice. Thus for 14 years Wojciech held the post

at that church in a laudable manner, and was held in high regard by all, for his wisdom, demonstrated at every chancellery function, and his piety. Besides this, he founded the collegiate church in Warsaw, and the cathedral.

Wojciech, also founded a city, having cleared some woods, and called it Jastrzebie. He endowed and gave to it two parish churches in Sandomierz province: one in Wysokie, in Lublin district; the other in Kortynicak, in Sandomierz district. He designated a tithe for the altar of St. Agnes, in Kraków diocese. Then in 1423, he was elevated to the rank of metropolitan and primate, and there left a memory of his generosity, funding two benefices, one theological and one juridical, as well as a third in Kalisz. He set up an altar in Leczyca, returned regular canons to Klodawa, and raised their church to collegiate rank. He died in 1436, an important, judicious man and a great lover of his country, favorably remembered and praised. Note that in Poland's 15th Century, the Archbishop of Gniezno not only controlled the entire Archdiocese but the entire realm, as dictated by the Papal Bull of Gniezno of 1136. (Excerpt and banner from Wikipedia; accessed 11/17/2024.)

Town or city	Babice, Chrzanów County
Country	Poland
Coordinates	🌐 50.0769°N 19.4447°E
Construction started	13th century

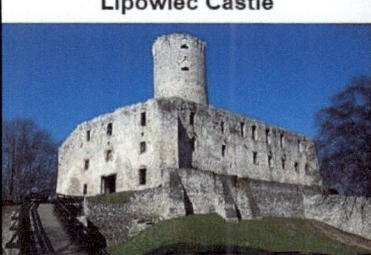

Lipowiec Castle

Perched on a hill in southern Poland, Lipowiec Castle ruins take you back to medieval times. Even though this once-mighty fortress has seen devastation by fires, it still retains significant parts of its structure. You can learn about its history as a prison and fortification at the museum, and climb the tower for spectacular views of forests and valleys.

The castle's present shape was developed in the 15th century by Wojciech Jastrzębiec (1412-1423) and Zbigniew Oleśnicki (1423-1451). Since the late 15th century the castle was used as a prison for ecclesiastical offenders.

Lipowiec Castle [1]

1485

1835 [2]

Jastrzebiec-Rytwiany Castle (The Bishop's Castle) [3]

In 1414, Wojciech Jastrzębiec acquired the local estate in Rytwiany for the castellans, and the castle itself was rebuilt in the first half of the 15th century at the bishop's expense, becoming the family residence of the Jastrzębiec-Rytwiański family. Only the fortified tower remains after a long history, though the monk's church is still active as a local parish church. The last owners of the village built a palace there, and in 2005, it was re-modeled as a resort hotel pictured below.

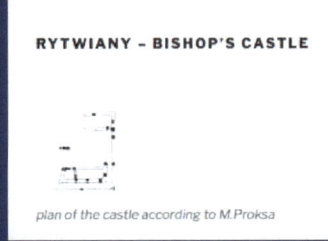

REFERENCES:
1. ©1997-2024 Viator, Inc. <www.viator.com/Krakow-attractions/Lipowiec-Castle/overview/d529-a20922>; accessed 11/23/2024.
2. J.N. Glacki lithography (1838) shows fire damage from 17th century attack by Swedish invaders when Poland drove them away.
3. Jastrzebiec Castle reported in <medievalheritage.eu/en/main-page/heritage/poland/rytwiany-bishops-castle>; accessed 11/23/2024.

Land Areas Developed by Jastrzębiec

Motto(s):	Jastrzębie-Zdrój – city of youth, work and peace
Coordinates:	49°57′N 18°35′E
Country	Poland
Voivodeship	Silesian
County	city county
Established	14th century
City rights	1963

Jastrzębie Zdrój, city, Śląskie *województwo* (province), southern Poland. Joined by the cities of Racibórz and Rybnik, Jastrzębie Zdrój forms a secondary industrial zone within the Upper Silesian area that borders the Czech industrial region of Ostrava.

Historically, Jastrzębie-Zdrój gained prominence as a spa town in the 19th century, attracting visitors seeking the healing properties of its mineral waters. Today, it continues to be a destination for wellness tourism while also offering a variety of attractions that cater to diverse interests. The city's unique blend of historical landmarks, cultural institutions, and natural beauty makes it a must-visit destination in Poland.

The history of Jastrzębie-Zdrój as a health resort came to its end in the 1960s, when all over the area began the intensive exploitation of coking coal deposits. Within a period of 12 years, five coal mines were set up. Between 1954–1975, Jastrzębie was part of the Wodzisław County. From 1975 to 1998, it was administratively located in the Katowice Voivodeship. During the time of political transformation in Poland, Jastrzębie-Zdrój went down the annals of Polish modern history as the place where the so-called "the Jastrzębskie Agreement" was concluded. The signing of the protocol initiated the process of political, economic and social changes in Poland.

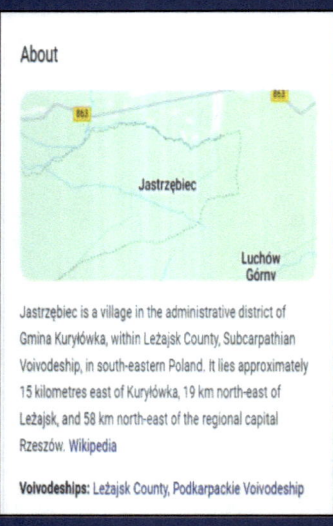

Jastrzębiec is a village in the administrative district of Gmina Kuryłówka, within Leżajsk County, Subcarpathian Voivodeship, in south-eastern Poland. It lies approximately 15 kilometres east of Kuryłówka, 19 km north-east of Leżajsk, and 58 km north-east of the regional capital Rzeszów. Wikipedia

Voivodeships: Leżajsk County, Podkarpackie Voivodeship

Jastrzębiec		Jastrzębie	
Village		Village	
Coordinates:	52°50′30″N 15°3′4″E	Coordinates:	53°13′N 19°31′E
Country	Poland	Country	Poland
Voivodeship	Lubusz	Voivodeship	Kuyavian-Pomeranian
County	Gorzów	County	Brodnica
Gmina	Lubiszyn	Gmina	Bartniczka
Population	60	Population	640

REFERENCES (excerpts):

1. Geographic description cited from Britannica (11/29/2024). <https://britannica.com/place/Silesia>; accessed 12/07/24.

2. Tobey, J. (2024) ©2024 Polish Culture NYC. *Things to do in Jastrzebie-Zdroj, Poland.* <https://polishculture-nyc.org/things-to-do-in-jastrzebie-zdroj-poland>; accessed 12/07/24.

3. Homer, M. (2024). History of Jastrzebie-Zdroj as a health resort. <https://thebastion.com/index_2.php?location=jastrzebie_zdroj>; accessed 12/07/24.

Coordinates:	50°03′13.6″N 19°12′04″E
Country	Poland

Jastrzebski Areas of Poland

Jastrzębiec

Article   Talk

From Wikipedia, the free encyclopedia

Jastrzębiec may refer to the following places:

- Jastrzębiec, Włocławek County in Kuyavian-Pomeranian Voivodeship (north-central Poland)
- Jastrzębiec, Sępólno County in Kuyavian-Pomeranian Voivodeship (north-central Poland)
- Jastrzębiec, Świętokrzyskie Voivodeship (south-central Poland)
- Jastrzębiec, Subcarpathian Voivodeship (south-east Poland)
- Jastrzębiec, Masovian Voivodeship (east-central Poland)
- Jastrzębiec, Greater Poland Voivodeship (west-central Poland)
- Jastrzębiec, Lubusz Voivodeship (west Poland)

See also   [edit]

- Jastrzębiec coat of arms

Jastrzębski Klif

Jastrzębia Gora

Jastrzebie-Zdroj Historic Spa

Jastrzębiec Lezajsk County Podkarpackie Voivodeship

Lex Zborowski

EVOLVING POWER STRUCTURE IN THE 16TH CENTURY

Zborowski's execution led to the adoption of a law in 1588, known as 'Lex Zborowski'. This law introduced the principle of procedure in cases concerning the crime of insulting the majesty in favor of the voting legislature.

The Zborowski Family

Marcin Zborowski

Marcin Zborowski of the Jastrzębiec coat of arms, lord of Oleśnica, representative of one of the oldest and most distinguished Polish families, had seven sons. With the exception of two: Marcin, who died young, and our Samuel, the rest made excellent careers at court. Piotr held the office of voivode of Kraków, Jan – castellan of Gniezno, Andrzej – court marshal of Henry Valois, Krzysztof – cup-bearer of the crown.[1]

Samuel Zborowski

It was during the coronation of Henry Valois at Wawel (in 1574), a quarrel broke out between Samuel and the castellan of Wojnicz, Jan Tęczyński. The castellan of Przemyśl, Andrzej Wapowski, tried to separate the combatants. The hot-tempered Samuel dealt him a blow to the head with an axe. As it turned out, it was fatal. As a result, he was sentenced to banishment by the king. In exile in Transylvania, he went to the Zaporozhian Sich, where as a Cossack hetman (military commander) he took part in the war with Russia in 1580.

In the summer of 1583, without the king's consent, he set off to Turkish lands, destroying Jahorlik and Tiahin, which belonged to Jan Zamoyski, in the process. This caused a deterioration in relations with Sultan Murad III, who threatened war if the guilty were not punished. When at the end of April 1584 Samuel Zborowski marched armed to his beloved niece in Piekary, not hiding that the destination of the expedition was Kraków, Jan Zamoyski issued an order to execute the decree of 1574, unprecedented in the history of law enforcement in noble Poland. On May 11, 1584 Samuel Zborowski was captured in Piekary, imprisoned as a dangerous criminal in the tower of Wawel Castle, and later famously beheaded.[2]

In Polish history, the king sentencing a magnate to death was an unprecedented event. The execution of Samuel Zbrowoski led the Polish Sejm (the Polish lower legislative chamber) to develop the concept of *liberum veto*. In Polish history, the legal right of each member to defeat by his vote alone any measure under consideration or to dissolve the Sejm and nullify all acts passed during its session. Based on the assumption that all members of the Polish nobility were absolutely equal politically, the veto meant, in practice, that every bill introduced into the Sejm had to be passed unanimously. This practice would come to be known as **Lex** (law) **Zborowski**.

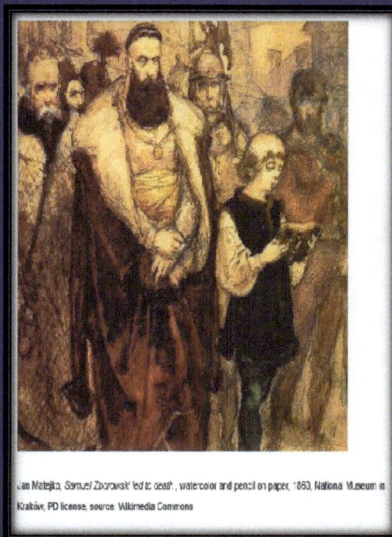

Jan Matejko, Samuel Zborowski led to death, watercolor and pencil on paper, 1860, National Museum in Kraków, PD license, source: Wikimedia Commons

According to the monographer of the Zborowski family, Dr. Ewa Dubas-Urwanowicz," Marcin [...] is a protoplast of the Jastrzębiec of "Rytwiany". His descendants used the name Rytwiańscy. Ścibor, instead, starts the line of later Jastrzębiecs "of Borysławice" and "of Zborów". [3]

Although legal, Zborowski's execution was quite irregular and outraged many in the nobility who perceived it a potential precedent for absolutism, causing the Sejm to enact *Lex Zborowski* to better govern the handling of treason cases. While issues arose from *liberum veto*, it was the beginning of the "Golden Liberty" established by the Sejm, a notable hallmark of the power structure within the Commonwealth, excluding the king as the decisive voice favoring the members of the legislature. Over time, Samuel himself became a symbol of the fight of a free citizen against tyranny.[4]

On July 1, 1569, the Sejm unanimously adopted that the kingdom of Poland and the grand principality of Lithuania were to be one inseparable and indivisible body politic. All dependencies and colonies, including Prussia and Livonia, were to belong to Poland and Lithuania in common.

Jan Matejko, Union of Lublin that created the Polish-Lithuanian Commonwealth National Museum in Lublin; source: CC BY-SA 3.0 / Wikimedia

REFERENCES:
1. As told by Pressmania.PL (2021) https://pressmania.pl/dumka-stepowa-czyli-pendolino/ © 2021 Pressmania; accessed 02/02/2025.
2. Ibid.
3. https://researchgate.net/publication/331912888 A few remarks on the history of the Zborowski family in the 16th century with reference to the book by Ewa Dubas-Urwanowicz; accessed 02/05/2025.
4. Posted by Headsman (May 26, 2018). http://executedtoday.com/2018/05/26/1584-samuel-zborowski-dangerousprecedent/; accessed 02/02/2025.

Szlachta During the Polish-Lithuanian Commonwealth

Golden Liberty

Szlachta elected the monarch by vote through their parliament and had veto power over the king's edicts.

Szlachta in costumes of the Voivodeships of the Crown of the Kingdom of Poland, Grand Duchy of Lithuania and the Polish-Lithuanian Commonwealth in the 17th and 18th century. / Krakow Museum, Wikimedia Commons

The term "szlachta" became the proper term for Polish nobility around the 15th century. The szlachta were the noble class in Poland and the Grand Duchy of Lithuania and acted as warriors and in parliament. The szlachta's dominance over the monarch was unprecedented in contemporary Europe. Further, as they protected the Commonwealth as invaders would come, they also protected the people, and themselves, from monarchical abuse. Though the use of titles was eliminated in the public arena under Poland's March 1921 Constitution, one's szlachta clan remains widely claimed in various strata of Polish society at home and abroad. (Citing inter alia Polska FM (2024). *Polish noble traditions: the Szlachta*. <https://polska.fm/polish-noble-traditions-the-szlachta>; accessed 12/09/2024.)

V·T·E	🇵🇱 Coats of arms of Polish–Lithuanian Commonwealth noble families	[hide]
Szlachta	Abdank · Abgarowicz · Achinger · Aksak · Alabanda · Alemani · Allan · Amadej · Antoniewicz · Azulewicz · Bajbuza · Belina · Bełty · Bes · Beztrwogi · Białynia · Biberstein · Bieńkowski · Biliński · Bogdanowicz · Bogorya · Bogusz · Bojcza · Bończa · Boreyko · Bożawola · Brama · Brochwicz · Brodzic · Brzuska · Casafranca · Chodkiewicz · Cholewa · Chyliński · Cieleski · Ciołek · Czarnowron · Czartoryski · Czewoja · Czewoja II · Dąb · Dąbrowa · Dąbrowski · Dąbrowski I · Dębno · Denhof · Deszpot · Dołęga · Doliwa · Drogosław · Druck · Drużyna · Dryja · Działosza · Finke · Fleming · Garczyński · Gąska · Geysztor · Giejsz · Gierałt · Ginwiłł · Glaubicz · Gliński · Godziemba · Goły · Gozdawa · Grabie · Grabowiec · Groty · Gryf · Gryzima · Grzymała · Gutak · Gwiazdy · Gwiaździcz · Haller · Hełm · Herburt · Hipocentaur · Hodyc · Hornowski · Hozyusz · Iwanowski · Janina · Jasieńczyk · **Jastrzębiec** · Jelita · Jeż · Juńczyk · Junosza · Kierdeja · Kietlicz · Klamry · Komar · Konderski · Kopacz · Lew II · Kopaszyna · Korab · Korczak · Korsak · Korwin · Korybut · Kościesza · Kot morski · Kotwica · Kotwicz · Kownia · Kozłowski · Kropacz · Krucina · Krukowski · Kryszpin · Krzywda · Księżyc · Kur · Kur II · Kurowski · Kusza · Łabędź · Larysza · Leliwa · Leszczyc · Lewart · Lis · Łodzia · Lubicz · Łuk · Mądrostki · Masalski Książę III · Materna · Mniszech · Mogiła · Mohyła · Mora · Nabram · Nałęcz · Napiwon · Nieczuja · Niesobia · Nowina · Nycz · Odrowąż · Odwaga · Odyniec · Ogończyk · Oksza · Orda · Oria · Osek · Ossorya · Ostoja · Ostroga · Ostrogski · Oszyk · Paprzyca · Pierzchała · Piłsudski · Piława · Pobóg · Pogoń Litewska · Pogoń Ruska · Pogonia · Półkozic · Pomian · Poraj · Pół Orła · Poronia · Pożniak · Prawdzic · Prus · Prus II Wilczekosy · Prus III · Przegonia · Przerowa · Przyjaciel · Przykorwin · Radwan · Rawa · Roch III · Rogala · Rola · Rosyniec · Rozmiar · Ryc · Samson · Sandrecki · Sas · Sas II · Starykoń · Sulima · Szreniawa · Topór · Trąby · Trestka · Wadwicz · Waga · Warnia · Wąż · Wczele · Wejher · Wieniawa · Wierzbna · Wilcza Głowa · Wysocki · Wyssogota · Zabawa · Zadora · Zagłoba · Zaremba · Zawadzki · Zerwikaptur · Zgraja	
	See also: Polish heraldry and List of Polish coat of arms	

Jastrzebski During the Polish-Lithuanian Commonwealth (1569-1795)

On July 1, 1569, the Union of Lublin was concluded, uniting Poland and Lithuania into a single, federated state, which was to be ruled by a single, jointly selected sovereign, responsive to a Senate and House of Deputies in a three Estate Sejm (parliament).

The princely houses of Poland and Lithuania differed from other princely houses in Europe. The Polish and Lithuanian nobility (szlachta) were not granted noblity titles by the King in the Polish-Lithuanian Commonwealth. Therefore, the title of prince either dated to the times before the Union of Lublin, which created the Commonwealth in 1569, or was granted to some by foreign kings. Further, some noble families often described as 'Polish' actually originated in Grand Duchy of Lithuania and are Lithuanian or Ruthenian descent, or more correctly described as being of the Polish-Lithuanian Commonwealth.* Below are Coat of Arms identified from the House of Jastrzębiec during this period featuring the goshawk with the horseshoe, with modifications to the COA and related but different surname.

Polish—Lithuanian Commonwealth [edit]

#	Name	Coat of Arms	Title recognition	Estates	Remarks
"Ancient" Princely Houses (Rody „stare")					
6	Połubiński			family exists	
7	Łukomski			family exists	
23	Gonzaga-Myszkowski		1601	Ordynacja Pińczowska	title expired in 1727
24	Gonzaga-Myszkowski-Wielopolski		1729	Ordynacja Pińczowska	family exists

*Source: Wikipedia, Updated 09/2022. *Princely Houses of Poland and Lithuania*; accessed 07/29/2024.

Great Warriors: The Polish Winged Hussars

Notable Achievements

Jastrzebski History Part II

Through the Polish-Lithuanian Commonwealth: Late 16th Century through the Late 18th Century

Above: Painting of Polish Winged Hussars in The Battle of Vienna 1683 by Jan Matejko, 1883.
Polish Winged Hussar story excerpts from the Polish Greatness Blog.

These and many other brilliant military masterminds continue to fascinate the world, and have since been a source of awe and inspiration not only to historians but military leaders of each era. Alexander the Great, Hannibal, and Caesar have been lauded, among others, as "gifted strategists" by men such as Napoleon Bonaparte and Duke of Wellington. In fact, military academies today still teach many of their brilliant tactics.

But in the realm of war stories, there is but one great story which has always been omitted. It does not dwell on the victories of any one leader, but rather on the succession of victories by a lineage of great and noble warriors. The greatest army ever assembled in the history of mankind was an elite branch of the Polish cavalry. They quickly developed into one of the most formidable armies throughout Europe. During the Middle Ages they struck fear into the hearts of their enemies. Their conquests surpassed that of any predecessor and their military prowess was supreme and undefeated **for over 200 years**.

THEY WERE THE POLISH WINGED HUSSARS

To describe the Polish Hussars as an elite branch of the cavalry would be an understatement. Most of them were recruited from wealthier Polish and Lithuanian nobility, and were referred to as the "szlachta". Each "towarzysz", or "comrade" was responsible in assembling his own "poczet" or retenue, and several of these were combined to form a hussar banner or company. In the meantime, during the 16th century, the hussars in Hungary had replaced their heavy wooden shields with full body metal armour. After the election of Stephen Batory as King of Poland (1575) and later acceptance of him as Grand Duke of Lithuania (1576), Batory re-organized the hussars of his Royal Guard to be equipped along the same lines as those of the Hungarian regiments, and equipped his men with long lances as their primary weapon. By the 1590s this transformation to heavy armor was all but complete and the Polish regiment became known as the "husaria".

Nevertheless, so fierce were the hussars that many of the Russian foreign mercenaries began deserting and joined the Polish forces. That event, and the fact that a large number of native Russians also began deserting their posts, greatly diminished the morale of the remaining Russian forces. Eventually, the Russian cavalry launched a counterattack but were heavily mauled by the Polish hussars. After a brief melee, the Russians broke ranks and fled in panic, suffering extensive losses.

The Polish Hussars' half-armour, mid-17th century at the National Museum in Kraków. (Wikimedia Commons)

A heavily armored Polish Hussar.

Thousands of winged hussars fought in the Battle of Klushino, helping to lead the Polish-Lithuanian forces to victory.

Story excerpts from the Polish Greatness Blog. Find more of the story at:
polishgreatness.blogspot.com/2011/06/great-polish-warriors-winged-hussars.html
Copyright 2010-2012 Polish Greatness (Blog). Awesome Inc.; accessed 10/20/2024.

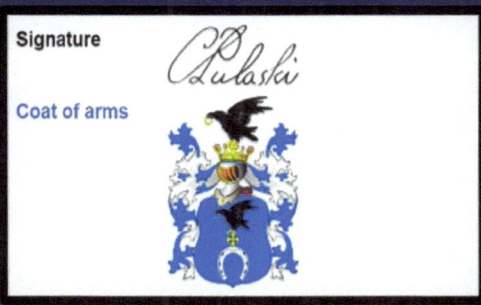

House of Jastrzębiec

Commander Casimir Pulaski
Winged Hussar Leader and American Revolutionary War Hero
Exiled from Partitoned Poland in 1772

Lineage

Kasimierz (Casimir) Pulaski was born in Podolia, Poland on 4 March 1747, son of Count Josef Pulaski, a member of the minor Polish gentry. He came from a family of knightly traditions - mostly warfare. Pulaski's family fought under Poland's King John III Sobieski against the Turks in the 17th century – a campaign that saved Europe. At the siege of Vienna in September 1683, the decisive battle of the campaign, the famed Polish winged hussars, heavily armored lancers, charged home against a mighty Turkish host and sent it in a retreat that would eventually begin the long decline of the Ottoman Empire. It was from the line of these bold horsemen that Pulaski sprang.

Charge of Winged Hussars at Vienna

Lineage cited from: yankeedoodlespies.blogspot.com/2019/03/polish-bad-ass-in-war-that-saw-many-bad.html. Painting of Pulaski by Jan Styka circa 1900. (Note that 'Jan' is the Polish spelling for 'Jon' or 'John'.)

Commander Casimir Pulaski: Polish Winged Hussars
1745-1779

Pulaski leading forces of the Bar Confederation at Czestochowa in 1771

Statue of Pulaski in Warka, Poland

Pulaski's achievements are recognized in Poland as well as the U.S.

Born in Warsaw and following in his father's footsteps, he became interested in politics at an early age. He soon became involved in the military and in revolutionary affairs in the Polish–Lithuanian Commonwealth. Pulaski was one of the leading military commanders for the Bar Confederation and fought against the Commonwealth's foreign domination. When this uprising failed, he was driven into exile.

Following a recommendation by Benjamin Franklin, Pulaski traveled to North America to help in the American Revolutionary War. He distinguished himself throughout the revolution, most notably when he saved the life of George Washington. Pulaski became a general in the Continental Army, and he and his friend, Michael Kovats, created the Pulaski Cavalry Legion and reformed the American cavalry as a whole. At the siege of Savannah, while leading a cavalry charge against British forces, he was fatally wounded by grapeshot and died shortly after.

Excerpt from Wikipedia, accessed 10/11/2024

Casimir Pulaski monument in Savannah, Georgia.

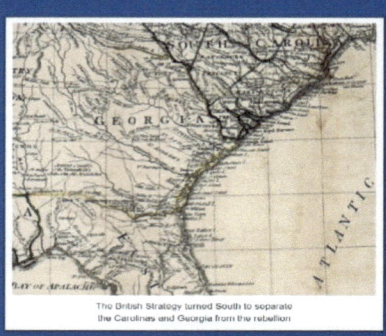

The British Strategy turned South to separate the Carolinas and Georgia from the rebellion

Final resting place of Gen. Pulaski in Savannah, Georgia, U.S.A.
Photo of Pulaski statue in Warka, Poland © 2024 Beata Bruggeman-Sekowska.

Illinois enacted a law on September 13, 1977, to celebrate the birthday of Casimir Pulaski and held the first official Pulaski Day celebrations in 1978. Today, Casimir Pulaski Day is celebrated mainly in areas with large Polish populations, including in Chicago, Bloomington and Du Bois, according to Northwestern University Polish Studies.

In 2009, President Barack Obama signed a joint resolution granting Pulaski honorary American citizenship, over 200 years after his death. He's one of only eight people to ever receive the honor.

Continental Army General and Commander of Pulaski's Legion

Pulaski, with Washington and Congress's approval, raised a new regiment of cavalry, along with a few regiments of infantry, which came to be known as Pulaski's Legion. Pulaski chose many of his officers and was able to train his legion as he saw fit. They rapidly became a dangerous force as Pulaski capitalized on his experience, creating some of America's first effective cavalry.

Stationed in Charleston, South Carolina, Pulaski became one of the leading commanders in the South. Upon his arrival in May 1779, Pulaski and Colonel John Laurens talked the terrified city leaders back from the brink of surrender to the British. Though Pulaski's Legion suffered heavy losses over the course of the war, they remained essential to the military in the South.

Pulaski's last engagement was during the Second Battle of Savannah on October 9, 1779, as the British sieged the city. Notified of the American plans by an informant, the British were prepared for the attack. As the tide quickly turned against the Americans, Pulaski led an assault against the British position hoping to drive a wedge between the British troops to regain the advantage.

He was wounded during the attack and, though his troops secured his body during the retreat, he died some days later from his injuries.

Excerpt above from the Digital Encyclopedia of George Washington ©2025.
www.mountvernon.org/library/digitalhistory/digital-encyclopedia/article/casimir-pulaski;
accessed 07/23/2025.

"I came here, where freedom is being defended, to serve it, and to live or die for it."
--General Casimir Pulaski to General George Washington

Casimir Pulaski, born in 1745 in Warsaw, then part of the Polish-Lithuanian Commonwealth, is celebrated as a hero in both Poland and the United States. His remarkable journey led him from fighting against partitioning powers in Poland to becoming a pivotal figure in the American Revolutionary War. Often referred to as the "Father of the American Cavalry," Pulaski's legacy is a testament to his unwavering commitment to the cause of liberty.

Pulaski's early involvement with the Bar Confederation in 1767, where he opposed Russian forces' presence in the Commonwealth, showcased his dedication to the pursuit of freedom. However, by 1772, he became disillusioned with the Confederation's leadership and left Poland for Prussia, under the warning of the Polish king to stay away.

His life took a momentous turn in 1777 when he attempted to join the French military but was recruited by none other than Benjamin Franklin and Lafayette. Impressed by Pulaski, Franklin recommended him to George Washington. Upon joining the Continental Army, Pulaski was granted the rank of brigadier general in the cavalry.

Pulaski's impact was swift and profound. He reformed the cavalry and led them to numerous successful campaigns. His heroism reached its pinnacle in October 1779 when he valiantly led an assault against British forces in Savannah, Georgia. Though wounded in the battle, Pulaski's courage and sacrifice for the American cause were undeniable.

It was on October 11th, 1779, that Casimir Pulaski passed away, leaving behind a legacy that continues to inspire. His story is a reminder of the unyielding spirit of those who dedicate their lives to the pursuit of liberty and justice. As we commemorate the anniversary of his death, we honor a hero who transcended borders and time, leaving an enduring mark on history.

Several U.S. States honor Pulaski's birth

Pulaski depicted in American art

Read about Pulaski's gift to U.S.

Casimir Pulaski is commemorated annually in the U.S. On the anniversary of his death since 1931

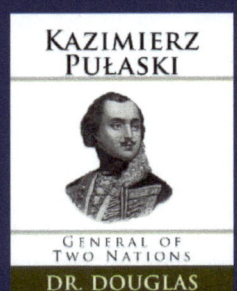

General Pulaski Memorial Day

Observed by	United States
Type	National Holiday
Date	October 11

A Proclamation on General Pulaski Memorial Day, 2024

BRIEFING ROOM • STATEMENTS AND RELEASES

Today, we pay tribute to General Casimir Pulaski, a Polish immigrant who served alongside American soldiers in the Revolutionary War and made the ultimate sacrifice for our Nation. And we honor the culture and contributions of all our Nation's Polish Americans who follow his legacy, standing up for the cause of freedom at home and around the world.

General Pulaski dedicated his life to the pursuit of liberty — not just for himself or his country but for all of us. Born and raised in Warsaw, Poland, he fought against the Russian domination of Poland — efforts that ultimately led him to flee his home country. Later in life, when he was offered an opportunity to join another fight for liberty on the other side of the world, he took it — joining our Nation's fight for independence. General Pulaski's service was critical: He led a critical counterattack that helped slow the British, and during the course of the war, it was said that he even saved George Washington's life.

General Pulaski's story and service are just one example of how much Polish Americans have shaped our Nation's history and our future. Our country's Polish-American communities have helped create new possibilities for all of us — leading in every sector, powering our economy, and enriching our culture. They also strengthen our deep alliance and partnership with Poland and its people at a critical time in our history. Since Russia's brutal invasion of Ukraine, the people of Poland have courageously stood up for freedom, liberty, and justice, rallying around the Ukrainian people and offering them safety and light in their darkest moments. At the same time, Poland has donated tanks, artillery, and aircraft to support Ukraine's self-defense all while becoming an important hub for aid from key partners.

Casimir Pulaski was a Polish nobleman who became a **brigadier** general in the **Continental** Army during the **American Revolutionary War**. One of the **United States'** first cavalry commanders, **Pulaski** brought organization and proper training to the Continentals, securing the titles of
"The Father of American Cavalry"
and
"Soldier of Liberty."

Chicago celebrates the birthday of Casimir Pulaski

Jastrzebski brothers Leonard Jaster and Ernest Jaski

Authorities and spokesmen on Pulaski

Casimir Pulaski Day is a holiday in Illinois that honors a Polish cavalry soldier in the American Revolutionary War.

Celebrated on the first Monday of March, Casimir Pulaski Day is a commemorative holiday. The day is meant to recognize Pulaski as a war hero but also to acknowledge the contributions that Polish Americans have made to the state and the nation.

The Last Great Victory
Defending the Commonwealth 1794

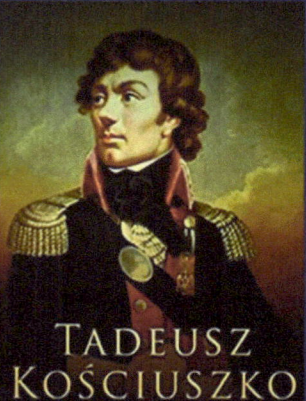

Kosciuszko also distinguished himself as a military commander fighting on behalf of the Colonials in the American Revolutionary War and, in 1794, became the leader of a national uprising in Poland. In his will, Kosciuszko bequeathed a large sum of money for the purpose of liberating and educating African-American slaves through his friendship with Thomas Jefferson. It was not possible to implement this testamentary request in the U.S. at that time, but Kosciuszko openly supported the end of slavery.

(Excerpt from *UVA Today*, 03/08/2011. https://news.virginia.edu/content/thomas-jefferson-and-polish-patriot-thaddeus-kosciuszko-are-topic-uva-talk-march-25>; accessed 12/21/2024.)

THE BATTLE THAT GAVE HOPE TO POLES

On 4 April 1794, the Polish army defeated the Russians in the Battle of Racławice. The victory primarily had a symbolic dimension and showed the strength and unity of the nation. It enabled the Kosciuszko Uprising to spread to other regions and became indelibly inscribed in the collective memory of Poles.

by Piotr Bejrowski

Prayer Before the Battle: Racławice by Józef Chełmoński, photo: National Museum in Wrocław

Three Partitions of Poland 1795

'Year 1863 – Polonia Enchained' by Jan Matejko, photo: Wikimedia

According to the traditional interpretation, the woman in white being separated from Polonia is Ruthenia, whilst the dead body lying in a pool of blood belongs to Lithuania.

City of Warsaw between 1890-1900. Photos via... - lamus dworski

HistoricalFindings Photo: Nicolaus Copernicus Monument, Staszic, Warsaw, Poland, 1895

While the szlachta remained influential in Polish society during the partitions, their political power was greatly diminished. Many nobles participated in **uprisings** against foreign rule in the 19th century, and the szlachta became a symbol of Polish resistance and patriotism during this period.

The three partitions of Poland, which took place in 1772, 1793, and 1795 respectively, were devastating for the Polish people. They also marked a turning point in European history in terms of nationalism and imperialism. The partitioning was a result of political, economic, and social factors that had been brewing in Europe for several decades. Prior to the sequence of annexations, Poland was a large and powerful state that had been weakened by conflict within its borders and external pressures from neighboring states. Spotting opportunity, several major geopolitical players in Europe decided to pounce on the advantage – citing the rich trove of resources within Polish borders, as well as its strategic location in the middle of the continent.

REFERENCES:

1. ©2024 Polska.fm. *Polish Noble Traditions: The Szlachta*. https://polska.fm.Polish-noble-traditions-the-szlachta; accessed 12/14/2024.

2. *Standjofski*, A. The 3 partitions of Poland & Lithuania: Polarized Peoples. The Collector 11/22/2023. Thecollector.com/Partitions-of-poland-and-lithuania; accessed 12/01/2024.

Related Families with the Jastrzebiec Coat of Arms
as of the 19th Century

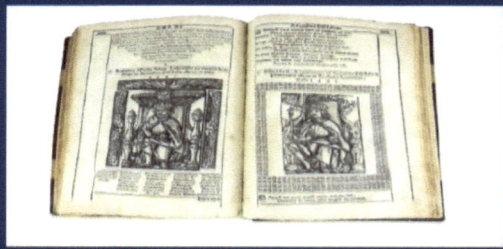 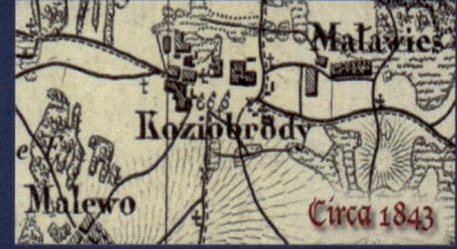

The following was prepared from the classic heraldic reference *Herbarz Polski* by Kasper Niesiecki, S. J., Lipsk [Leipzig] edition, 1839-1846; excerpt from Polishroots.com, page id 176.

For further information on Polish families by Coat of Arms see Polish Roots® Polish Genealogical Records @ polishroots.com or the Polish Genealogical Society of America®, pgsa.org.

Families Using these Arms

Abrahamowicz, Adamowski, Albinowski

Balinski, Baranowski, Bartoszewski, Bedzislawski, Bekierski, Beldowski, Belkowski, Belzecki, Beski, Biejkowski, Bielewski, Bierczynski, Bninski, Bobrowski, Boguslawski, Bolesz, Borowski, Boruta, Brodecki, Bromirski, Brudkowski, Brudnicki, Brzechfa, Brzeski, Brzezicki, Brzozowski, Brzuchanski, Budkowski, Bukowski, Bylecki, Byszewski

Charbicki, Chelstowski, Chmielecki, Chmielowski, Chochol, Chorczewski, Choszczewski, Chudkowski, Chwalibowski, Chwedkowicz, Chylewski, Chylinski, Cieklinski, Ciesielski, Cieszewski, Ciolkowski, Cudzinowski, Czajka, Czepowski, Czernicki, Czeski, Czeszowski

Dabrowski, Debowski, Dobrski, Domaradzki, Domaszewski, Doranski, Dragowski, Drochowski, Drozdowicz, Drozdowski, Dziebakowski, Dziegielowski, Dzierzgowski, Dziewanowski

Falecki

Gaszynski, Gembart, Geraltowski, Gibowski, Glinski, Gliszczynski, Gloskowski, Godziszewski, Golanski, Golawski, Golocki, Gorecki, Gostynski, Goszycki, Grabkowski, Grabowski, Grazimowski, Grebecki, Grodecki, Grzebski, Grzywienski

Hermanowski, Hoholewski

Iwanski

Janikowski, Jankowski, Janowski, Jasinski, Jastrzembecki, Jastrzembski, Jedrzejowski, Jeżewski, Jodlownicki, Jurkowski

Kaczynski, Kaminski, Karski, Karsznicki, Kepski, Kierski, Kierznowski, Klembowski, Kliszewski, Konarski, Konopnicki, Koperni, Koscien, Kosilowski, Kosmaczewski, Kosnowie, Koziebrodzki, Kozlowski, Krasowski, Krzesimowski, Krzywanski, Kucharski, Kuczkowski, Kudbryn, Kukowski, Kul, Kuropatwa, Kuźmicki,

Lawdanski, Lazicki, Lazienski, Leszczynski, Letkowski, Lukomski, Lutomirski, Lysakowski

Maciejowski, Maczynski, Makomeski, Malewski, Maloklecki, Maluski, Mankowski, Marszewski, Maszkowski, Matczynski, Mayer, Miedzyleski, Mierzynski, Mietelski, Milanowski, Milewski, Mirski, Mniewski, Mojkowski, Mojski, Morski, Mysliszewski, Myszkowski

Nagora, Necz, Niedroski, Niegoszewski, Niemira, Niemsta, Niemyglowski, Niemyski, Niesmierski, Nieweglowski, Nowiewski, Nowomiejski, Nowowiejski

Oblow, Ocieski, Olizarowski, Olszanski, Orlowski, Osiecki

Paczowski, Pakosz, Papieski, Paprocki, Pawlowski, Pecławski, Pelczycki, Pelka, Peszkowski, Pilchowski, Pniewski, Polikowski, Polubinski kniaź, Poplawski, Porczynski, Poreba, Powczowski, Preisz, Przedpelski, Przedzynski, Przeradzki, Psarski

Rachanski, Racibor, Raczynski, Rebiecki, Rembiewski, Rodecki, Rogowski, Rozembarski, Roznowski, Rucki, Rudnicki, Rychlowski
Sadzynski, Sarnowski, Sasin, Sek, Siemietkowski, Skopowski, Skorycki, Skrzetuski, Skrzyszowski, Sladkowski, Slawecki, Slugocki, Smolski, Sokolnicki, Srokowski, Starczewski, Stawiski, Strzelecki, Strzembosz, Strzeszkowski, Stuzenski, Suchorski, Sulaczewski, Świecicki, Szaszewicz, Szczyt, Szeczemski, Szomanski, Szulenski, Szumski
Taczanowski, Tanski, Tlokinski, Tlubicki, Trzebinski, Trzepienski, Turlaj, Tynicki
Uchacz, Ulatowski
Wakczewski, Wawrowski, Wazenski, Weźyk, Wierzbicki, Wierzbowski, Wiewiecki, Wiktorowski, Witoslawski, Witowski, Wnuczek, Wodzinski, Wolecki, Wroblowski, Wydzga, Wyrozebski
Zadorski, Zakrzewski, Zalesicki, Zarski, Zawadzki, Zawidzki, Zawilski, Zawistowski, Zberowski, Zborowski, Zdan, Zdunowski, Zdzieszek, Żegocki, Żernowski, Zielonka, Zukowski, Żytkiewicz

Addition to Niesiecki's text by the 19th-century editor, J N. Bobrowicz
Later heraldists such as Kuropatnicki, Malachowski, Wieladek and others add the following:

Borejko, Brühl, Butkiewicz, Chilewski, Cieszcjowski, Grzegorzewski, Jezowski, Koczanski, Koczkowski, Kopeszy, Lemnicki, Lgocki, Mosakowski, Mszczuj, Nasiegniewski, Niemirowicz, Niemyglowski, Niezdrowski, Opatkowski, Paczynski, Pakowski, Palczycki, Pelczewski, Pet, Pininski, Protaszewicz, Przedpolski, Raciborowski, Rytwianski, Sasiewicz, Sasinski, Siemiatkowski, Skorczycki, Skorski, Skubajewski, Skubniewski, Skurski, Sulenski, Sumowski, Szczemski, Szczepkowski, Szwab, Tarnawiecki, Tlubinski, Trzeszewski, Waszkowski, Wolicki, Worainski, Wykowski, Wzdulski, Xiaźki, Zakowski, Zawadzicki, Zólkowski, Zub, Zub Zdanowicz.

Variations in Coat of Arms

Not all those listed here use the Jastrzebiec arms in the same form: some bear the Goshawk standing in a red field on two horseshoes, with three ostrich plumes on the helmet. With others the hawk or raven on the helmet holds a ring in its beak, not a horseshoe in its talons, for instance, Kierski, Konopnicki, and Lesczynski. The Rudnickis have the Goshawk holding a horseshoe in his beak on the helmet. In Miedzyrzycz near Ostróg I saw a coat of arms which had above the horseshoe and cross, as are usually seen in the Jastrzebiec arms, an added star, and on the helmet three ostrich plumes. On the headstone of Jan Rokiczana, pseudo-bishop of Prague, a horseshoe was shown, in its center was a star, not a cross, as Balbinus attests (book 5, chapter 10), but some say of him that he was a smith's son. Haubicki and Plachecki bear the hawk in another form, as is discussed under the letter H. The Niemyskis have an arrow inside the horseshoe, instead of a cross, with its head pointing straight up but split on the bottom. There are some who have a raven standing above the horseshoe and cross, with its beak pointing to the right side of the shield and holding a ring in in it, with the diamond pointing downward. Others place an arrow without feathers above the horseshoe, or on an apple, or on the world, with three ostrich plumes on the helmet, such as the Mirskis; each of these is discussed in its place. Others add a hunter's horn over the horseshoe, without attachments, with three ostrich plumes on the helmet, as for instance the Kierznowskis. Others place two arrows and a cross in the center of the horseshoe, as do the Szaszewiczes.   Others put three stars over the horseshoe, with three ostrich plumes on the helmet, as do the Turlajs.

The Resurrection of Poland 1918

The Resurrection of Poland by Władysław Barwicki, photo: Culture.pl

Great Polish Warriors of the 20th Century

Notable Achievements
Jastrzebski History Part III

Victory in WWI
Restoring Poland's National Sovereignty 1918

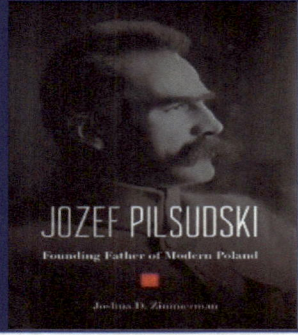  

On 11 November Poland celebrates the National Independence Day

  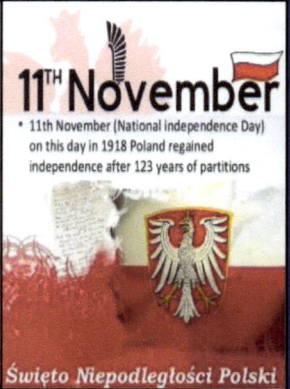

11th November 1918, Polish Legions Commander & Marshall Józef Piłsudski receiving a parade in front of the Bristol Hotel in Warsaw, photo: Piotr Mecik / FORUM

On 10th November 1918, Piłsudski comes to Warsaw, freed from Magdeburg by the Germans [he had been interned there after refusing to fight for Germany]. On the 11th, he takes control of the military. On the 14th, he receives full power. The discussion as to which date to recognise as the formal regaining of independence was a long one.

From an interview with Wiesław Wysocki, chairman of the Piłsudski Institute, published in 'Niepodległość', 2017, trans. MK

"November 11, as the anniversary of Poland regaining its independent existence and as a day forever associated with the great name of Józef Piłsudski, the nation's victorious leader in the struggle for the freedom of the motherland, is to be a solemn Independence Day."

Poland names the 11th of November as Independence Day in 1937 after Pilsudski's death

In November 1918, just two weeks after Poland regained independence, Polish women were granted the right to vote. Poland was among the first countries to achieve women's suffrage.

Citations @<polishatheart.com/11-november-origins-of-polands-national-independence-day>; accessed 11/11/24.

The Jastrząb and the Last of Partitioned Poland

July 18, 1918

Nearby Warsaw, the Polish army not only defended the independence of the Polish State, but also stopped the march of Bolshevik hordes on Europe.

REFERENCES: Zgorzelski, Rafat. *The Battle of Warsaw, 1920* (2020). ©Warsaw Institute, 10 Aug 2020. https://warsawinstitute.org/battle-warsaw-1920/; accessed 02/15/2025. Image of Pilsudski from https://images.app.goo.gl/UtMW2wQM4oUvnV3z7.

GOSHAWK
(*Accipiter genitilis*)

Back from the brink of extinction, the goshawk is the ultimate woodland predator. Its wings are tailor-made for weaving through trees and hunting almost anything it outsizes.

Jan Jastrzebski moves to Chicago in 1920, possibly as a clan preservation strategy.

Restoring national sovereignty was a big victory for Poland, but peace was short-lived. The emerging Soviet Union continues to attack Poland and in 1939, WWII begins with the German Nazi invasion of Poland. Nazis annihilate millions of Poles in WWII, millions of European Jews, as well as causing the toll of the war itself. After WWII ends in 1945, U.S. becomes a world power with a large diaspora of Poles in Chicago. Germany is divided by the Berlin Wall for 28 years and given food rations. Poland is burdened with Soviet occupation.

Communist and Post-Communist Studies (2021) 54 (4): 157–175.
https://doi.org/10.1525/j.postcomstud.2021.54.4.157

After World War II, Polish nobility was commonly considered an obsolete social group because of the post-1945 confiscation of their properties and the decline of their legal and political privileges. From a formal point of view, the Polish nobility had ceased to exist. However, this group did not simply vanish. For this reason, we should not speak of the disintegration of the former noble milieu but rather its reorganization. To expand deliberation on these "reorganization strategies" with the use of appropriate sociological tools, this article analyzes major social actors in contemporary Poland who use their noble legacies in their collective identity-building practices.

Two references for FURTHER READING about reorganization strategies of the Polish nobility shown above. Goshawk description from <The WoodlandTrust.uk.com>, accessed 09/29/2024.

The American Jastrzebski Clan Chicago
Saint Stanislaus Kostka Parish

Eva Czapska weds Jan Jastrzebski in 1922

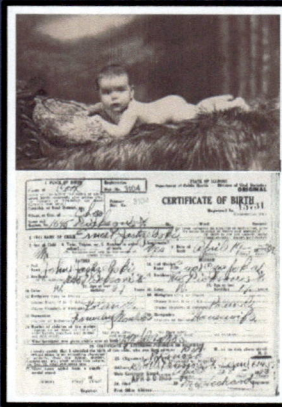

Early Years Jastrzebski 1920s Home on Bosworth Ave. First American-born Jastrzebskis Ernest, Leonard, Esther

Ernest born 1923   **Leonard born in 1924**   **Esther born in 1928**

"Family Market" was the Jastrzebski neighborhood store

Polish Museum of American opens 1937   *Zgoda* informs all of the homeland in Poland

WWII Begins in Poland 1939

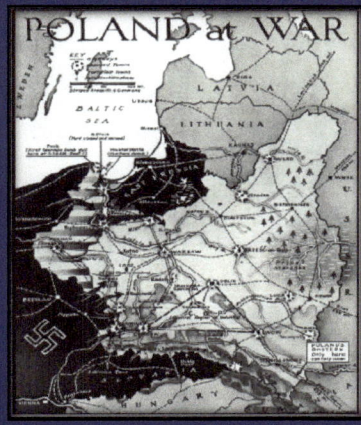

German Nazis destroy Jan & Eva Jastrzebski's

Gdansk was called "Danzig" during 1939-1945, when it was occupied by Nazi Germany, to simplify the pronunciation of the Polish name for the Germans. In 1945, when Germany was defeated again in WWII, the German population was expelled or vacated. Germany controlled Gdansk for a short period of time, then, during 1871-1918 and during the six years of Nazi occupation during WWII. Otherwise, it was a Polish territory since the 10th century.

family hometown of Gdansk

© 2024 LRE Foundation. The Last Days of the War in Gdansk. https://liberationroute.com/pois/211/the-last-days-of-the-war-in-gdansk; accessed 12/20/2024.

Chicago prepares for war

U.S. enters WWII in 1941. Chicago men and women fervently join the war effort against protagonists Germany and Japan, at home and abroad.

Ernest and Leonard Jastrzebski graduate from St. Stanislaus Kostka High School just in time for military conscription. They were assigned to different branches of the armed forces, serving until the wars end in 1945. While both sons were abroad, father Jan Jastrzebski dies. Neither son is permitted leave for the funeral.

U.S. Naturalization Record Indexes, 1791-1992 (Indexed in World Archives Project)

Name:	Eva Jastrzebski
Birth Date:	3 Aug 1903
Birth Place:	Poland
Age at event:	39
Court District:	Illinois, Indiana, Wisconsin, Iowa
Date of Action:	15 Dec 1942

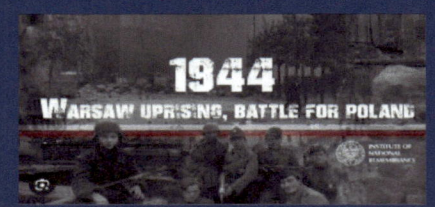

Warsaw Uprising

The monument commemorates the many Polish soldiers and civilians who lost their lives in battle and in prison camps resisting the German Nazi invasion single-handedly for 63 days. In WWII, Poland was assigned the Russian Soviet Union as an ally, essentially trading one assailant for another.

Casualties during the Warsaw Uprising were catastrophic. Although the exact number of casualties is unknown, it is estimated that about 16,000 members of the Polish resistance were killed and about 6,000 badly wounded. In addition, between 150,000 and 200,000 Polish civilians died, mostly from mass executions. About 85% of Warsaw was destroyed. (Source: National WWII Museum.) The Polish people rebuilt Warsaw on their own, only to be controlled by the Soviet Union after a victorious WWII.

Warsaw after the German invasion of 1944

Warsaw today with re-captured statue of Copernicus

V-E Day Victory in WWII 1945
Albina Czapska with cousin Ernest Jastrzebski at the Palmer House 1945

The Allied Responses to the Warsaw Uprising of 1944

The Warsaw Uprising created a rift between Stalin and his Western Allies, which some historians argue anticipated the Cold War.

Border adjustment between Poland and the USSR

On August 16, 1945, a border agreement between Poland and the USSR was signed. The

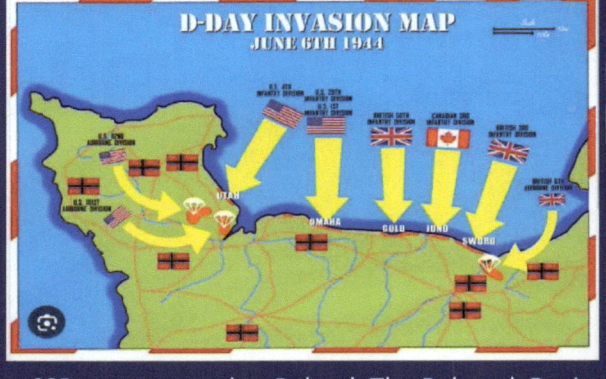

western portion of the Byelorussian SSR was restored to Poland. The Belastok Region was divided into Soviet Region, Grodno Region and Polish Białystok Voivodeship. Initially, at the end of World War II in 1945, Poland also gained control of the current southern border strip of the Kaliningrad Oblast, with Polish administration organized in the towns of Gierdawy and Iławka, however, the area was eventually annexed by the Soviet Union and included within the Kaliningrad Oblast by December 1945. As a result, Poland lost about 178,000 square kilometres (69,000 square miles) of its pre-war territory in the east, but gained some 101,000 square kilometres (39,000 square miles) in the west and north. Source: https://en.wikipedia.org/wiki//Territorial evolution of Poland; accessed 03/01/2025.

Roll of Honor Jastrzebski

Washington National Cathedral Honors U.S. WWII Veterans

Queen Elizabeth II and U.S. President Eisenhower open War Memorial Chapel
Washington National Cathedral 1957

Gary and father Leonard Jaster
At WWII Veteran Reunion in DC

HONOR FLIGHT for WWII Veterans
2008

Florence and Mailee Jaster
greet their return

Ernest Bernard Jastrzebski
U.S. Army Air Force European Theater (ETO)
Honorable Discharge Dec 1945

Leonard Thomas Jastrzebski
U.S. Navy Pacific Duty
Honorable Discharge Dec 1945

The First Generation in Chicago

The two adult sons were encouraged to simplify their Polish surname in the U.S. They did, and each chose different variations of the Jastrząb surname.

The Parish That Moved An Expressway - St. Stanislaus Kostka Parish | Church Open 24-7 - Chicago, IL

Eva Jastrzebski saw both her sons return from WWII and her daughter married. Though she died soon after, Eva had worked to maintain the family home where all three grown children, and their spouses, lived shortly after their marriages. In the 1950s, the Polish neighborhood was disrupted by the post-WWII commission of a major expressway (later named "the Kennedy"). Community outcry altered construction plans to accommodate the Polish parish church that remains open today. Many families, though, were required to sell their homes. After the sale of the Jastrzebski home, all three adult children purchased homes in other Chicago area locations.

Photo left: Ernest Jaski receives his Ph.D. in Education from the University of Chicago in the 1960s. In photo, Uncle Bernie Czapski, Esther, and the Jaski family.
Photo right: Rockefeller Chapel at the University of Chicago.

Jastrzebski Honored in 1962 as Rescuers of Jews

Foreign Minister Golda Meir speaks at the dedication ceremony

Title	Nationality	Rescue Places
Jastrzębska Maria (Sobertin); Son: Jastrzębski Bogdan	POLAND	Czestochowa, Czestochowa, Kielce, Poland; Warsaw, Warszawa, Warszawa, Poland
Lipszyc Aldona (Jastrzębska)	POLAND	Ostrówek, Warszawa, Poland; Warszawa, Warszawa, Warszawa, Poland
Ostrowska Janina ; Daughter: Krasucka Barbara (Ostrowska); Daughter: Jastrzębska Krystyna (Ostrowska); Sister: Siedlińska Brunona	POLAND	Chylice, Warszawa, Warszawa, Poland
Holland Irena (Rybczyńska)	POLAND	Chylice, Warszawa, Warszawa, Poland; Warszawa, Warszawa, Warszawa, Poland
Krakiewicz Janina (Czyzewska)	POLAND	Wlochy, Warszawa, Warszawa, Poland
Lis Helena ; Daughter: Władysława	POLAND	Lwow, Lwow, Lwow, Poland

The Avenue of the Righteous, Yad Vashem, 2007

The Jastrzeb Agreement 1980

Anniversary of the Jastrzębie Agreement

03.09.2024

44 years ago, one of the historic August Accords was signed - the Jastrzeb Agreement, which became a symbol of resistance against communist rule and the fight for workers' rights. Ceremonies commemorating those events were held today in front of the monument at the Zofiówka mine.

The third of September marks another anniversary of the signing of the Jastrzębie Agreement, concluded between the workers and the communist government, ending the wave of strikes of the summer of 1980. This is one of the three August Agreements, which were among the key events in Poland's post-war history. The anniversary ceremony in Jastrzębie-Zdrój was attended by Polish Prime Minister Mateusz Morawiecki.

Posted on 28 September 2018 Author Redaktor

Jastrzębie Agreement

On the last day of September 1980 the whole world looked upon the Gdańsk Shipyard. The Agreement between the communist regime and representatives of enterprises on strike became one of the most significant events in the history of our country. The content of this agreement is easily available for the public (though not as widely known as one would expect) but the whereabouts of the document itself (or of its two equal copies, one prepared for the government, the other for the workers) are lost in the mists of time, though not so remote.

Jastrzębie Coal Mine
Silesia

- Although the official founding of NSZZ "Solidarity" did not take place until November 1980, it was in fact established here. Through the great strike movement that began in mid-July in Lublin, Świdnik, through the strike in the shipyard and other plants that joined it, resulting in the formation of the Intercompany Strike Committee and, in turn, the Szczecin, Gdańsk, Jastrzębie and Dąbrowa agreements. All of this combined to create "Solidarity" - said the President of Poland, Andrzej Duda, also emphasizing how significant "Solidarity" really is:

– "Solidarity" does not want to rule, "Solidarity" upholds fundamental values. Those stemming from Catholic teachings, from the Decalogue, the inherent right of every human being to dignity and appropriate living conditions.

REFERENCES:
1. JSWA, (09 March 2022). *The 42nd Anniversary of the Jastrzebie agreement*. ©JSWA 2022.
2. Outriders Stories. *The Jastrzebie Coal Mine*. <https://outride.rs/en/articles/jastrzebie-coal-mine>; accessed 12/07/2024.
3. Institute of National Remembrance (08/20/2024). *Celebrating the 44th anniversary of the signing of the August agreements*. <https://eng.ipn.gov.pl/en/news/11448,Celebrating-the-44th-anniversary-of-the-signing-of-the-August-Agreements.html>, accessed 12/07/2024.
4. JSWA, (03 Sept 2023). *43 years since the signing of the historic agreement*. <https://jsw.pl/en/press-office/news/archive/archive-news-article/43-lata-od-podpisania-historycznego-porozumienia>; accessed 12/07/2024.

The Second Coming of Poland 1981-1989

Warsaw, December 1981. The First day of Martial Law. Kino Moskwa screens Francis Ford Coppola's 'Apocalypse Now', photo: Chris Niedenthal, press material

Pope John Paul II hugs Lech Walesa, leader of Poland's Solidarity trade union during his visit to the northern port of Gdansk, 11 June 1987. Photograph: Arturo Mari/AFP/Getty Images

The Nobel Peace Prize 1983 was awarded to Lech Wałęsa "for non-violent struggle for free trade unions and human rights in Poland"

"I believe that, sooner or later, the rights of individuals, of families, and of entire communities will be respected in every corner of the world."

LECH WALESA
Nobel Peace Prize 1983

Lech Walesa: The Leader of Solidarity and Campaigner for Freedom and Human Rights in Poland (People Who Have Helped the World)

Craig, Mary

Note: This is not the actual book cover

At their first meeting, Reagan and John Paul II discussed something else they had in common: both had survived assassination attempts only six weeks apart in 1981, and both believed God had saved them for a special mission.

"We both felt that a great mistake had been made at Yalta and something should be done," Reagan says today. "Solidarity was the very weapon for bringing this about, because it was an organization of the laborers of Poland. Nothing quite like Solidarity had ever existed in Eastern Europe...."

The operation was focused on Poland, the most populous of the Soviet satellites in Eastern Europe and the birthplace of John Paul II. Both the Pope and the President were convinced that Poland could be broken out of the Soviet orbit if the Vatican and the U.S. committed their resources to destabilizing the Polish government and keeping the outlawed Solidarity movement alive after the declaration of martial law in 1981.

According to U.S. intelligence sources, the Pope had already advised Walesa through church channels to keep his movement operating underground, and to pass the word to Solidarity's 10 million members not to go into the streets and risk provoking Warsaw Pact intervention or civil war with Polish security forces. Because the communists had cut the direct phone lines between Poland and the Vatican, John Paul II communicated with Jozef Cardinal Glemp in Warsaw via radio. He also dispatched his envoys to Poland to report on the situation. "The Vatican's information was absolutely better and quicker than ours in every respect," says Haig. "Though we had some excellent sources of our own, our information was taking too long to filter through the intelligence bureaucracy."

REFERENCES (excerpts):
1. Bernstein, Karl. (Feb 24, 1982). *The Holy Alliance: Ronald Reagan and Pope John Paul II* © 1992 Time Magazine. <https://time.com/archive/6719650/the-holy-alliance-ronald-reagan-and-john-paul-ii>; accessed 12/07/24.
2. The Guardian News and Media (11 June 1987). <https://theguardian.com/world/2020/jun/12/pope-in-open-challenge-to-poland-martial-law-archive-1987>; 12/07/24.

Photo credit: ©Giedymin Jablonski, 1980

Warsaw's Revenge:
Freedom for Poland 1989
Solidarity party ousts Soviet Communism in Poland and 15 other countries follow Poland's example. By 1991, the Soviet Union is dissolved.

1989 Roundtable Talks in Warsaw   **Ernest B. Jaski in Poland 1989**

On February 6, 1989, Communist officials launched the so-called Round Table Talks in Warsaw with Walesa's Solidarity and other opposition groups. Poland's Communists had hoped to bring opposition leaders into the fold without changing the political power structure. They failed, however. The Polish Round Table Agreement, signed on April 4, 1989, legalized independent trade unions and laid the way for a democratic government. The agreement is seen as lending momentum to the string of 1989 revolutions leading to the fall of the Communist bloc.

There are 15 post-Soviet states in total: Armenia, Azerbaijan, Belarus, Estonia, Georgia, Kazakhstan, Kyrgyzstan, Latvia, Lithuania, Moldova, Russia, Tajikistan, Turkmenistan, Ukraine, and Uzbekistan.

© 2024 RFE/RL Inc. <www.rferl.org/a/poland-walesa-turns-70-photos/25118425.html>; 11/02/2024.

The "Free White Eagle"

The Polonia Eagle returns to Poland's Flag

Poland joined the European Union on May 1, 2004, under the Accession Treaty signed on April 16, 2003, in Athens. As an EU member state, Poland influences the decisions made within the European Union.

Poland admitted to NATO in 1999 after several years of legal reforms

The House of Jastrzebski
The Next Generation

Marjorie, Blythe & Brian Jaski

Helene & Bernie Czapski in Florida

Ernest & Lori Jaski

Above: Tony and Esther Serek with daughter Cindy and her husband John Patzelt. Esther, grandmother of Tommy J. and Lisa and mother of Tom (on right) and Cindy. Esther dies in 1985, the only daughter of Jan and Eva Jastrzebski. Husband and father Tony Serek dies in 2009. John is a trade union activist in Chicago.

The Jasters Brothers
Len & Gary Jaster

Parents
Leonard & Florence
pictured below

Uncle Bernie with his shuffleboard "staff"

Bernie Czapski was the brother of Eva Czapska Jastrzebski and uncle to Ernest, Leonard, and Esther. He was a big help to his sister Eva after Jon, her husband, had died while the sons were abroad fighting in WWII. Later, Uncle Bernie hosted family gatherings every New Year's Day at his home in Northwest Chicago. When he retired, he married for the first time. He and his wife Helene moved to Fort Lauderdale, Florida, where Bernie became the Shuffleboard Champion of his community. Uncle Bernie died in 1983 and was buried in Hollywood, Florida next to his wife Helene.

Chicago commissions a replica of the Copernicus Statue in Warsaw in honor of the 500th anniversary of his birth in 1473.

Uncle Bernie is also remembered in Ernest's middle name and as Brian's godfather.

Photo left: Adler Planetarium in Chicago

The Story of the Harvest Moon Ball Dance Championship

When Ernest Jaski (born Jastrzebski) returned from Europe and WWII, at the age of 22, he moved in with his mother, brother, and sister in their 3-story walk-up in the Polish neighborhood of Chicago.

Ernest and his sister Esther enjoyed the local dance competitions that were held in the neighborhood--and they always won. They were encouraged to compete in the **Harvest Moon Ball Dance Championship**; the national dance competition held annually in Chicago. Ernest and Esther decided to go for it!

As Ernest recalled later, they arrived at the Registration Desk in their Sunday best. For Ernest, at the time, this was a plaid jacket and bow tie. It was then that Ernest and Esther were asked for their "credentials." It turned out, one cannot just enter the Harvest Moon Ball Dance Championship, but rather involves a series of preliminary competitions; entrance, dress, and other competition rules that must be adhered to well in advance.

Ernest and Esther returned to the neighborhood. Fortunately, over the years to follow, Ernest and his wife Lori frequently enjoyed dancing together, took lessons, and attended many dance competitions. But it wasn't until Lori died in February 2001 that Ernest revived his interest to compete in the Harvest Moon Ball Dance Championship. And, at age 78, that is exactly what he did.

Ernie & Lori Jaski at a dance party

**Harvest Moon Ball Dance Championship 1st Place Winners 2001
Ernest Jaski with dance partner Becky (his instructor)**

Education pioneer Ernest Jaski dies

By Carrie Wolfe
Staff writer

Education visionary and entrepreneur Ernest B. Jaski believed that education could unlock doors and bridge the gap between the American Dream and the real world, his family said.

"He just felt ... it was an honor both to teach and to be taught," Mr. Jaski's daughter, Marjorie Jaski McCarthy said.

Mr. Jaski, 79, of Oak Forest, died March 18 at Sharp Memorial Hospital in San Diego. He had cancer.

Mr. Jaski was instrumental in the development of what became the City Colleges of Chicago. He was a retired professor who taught business and marketing for most of his 33 years at Richard J. Daley College.

Mr. Jaski helped pioneer distant learning at City Colleges, in which students study via television courses, Jaski McCarthy, 43, said.

After retiring from the City Colleges, he served on the Educational Council of the Great Books Foundation and was the founding president of the Oak Lawn Library Foundation.

Mr. Jaski also was a member of the International Association of Educators for World Peace and developed peace education/conflict resolution courses and promoted peace education in travels to communist countries.

As chairman of the advisory board for Felician College, (later Montay College) in Chicago, he established the Peace Institute and adult education program, helping the Catholic women's college keep open its doors for another 20 years by transforming it into a working adults college.

After the Vietnam War, Mr. Jaski initiated a program to help integrate refugees from Southeast Asia in the Chicago area, helping hundreds of Laotian, Cambodian and Vietnamese immigrants to learn English and secure jobs, Jaski McCarthy said. The program was recognized with the Asian Forum award for its outstanding success.

Born in Chicago to Polish immigrants, Mr. Jaski lived in Oak Forest for the past 14 years and also lived in Oak Lawn, Downers Grove and Chicago's Beverly and Hyde Park communities.

He received his master's degree in business administration from Northwestern University and a doctorate from the University of Chicago.

For all of his community involvement, he also encouraged his kids to achieve, said Jaski McCarthy of Wilmette.

"He was very much devoted as a father to our education (so) that we would reach our own potential, which he considered unlimited," she said.

Mr. Jaski is survived by two daughters, Jaski McCarthy and Blythe McGarvie of Williamsburg, Va.; a son, Brian Jaski of San Diego; and a granddaughter, K.C. Jaski of San Diego.

A funeral service will be held at 10 a.m. today at St. Damian Church, 5220 155th St., Oak Forest.

Burial will be at St. Mary Cemetery in Evergreen Park.

Carrie Wolfe may be reached at cwolfe@dailysouthtown.com or (708) 633-5967.

Ernest Jaski knew all-too-well the challenges of pursuing an education while raising children, earning a living, and the time required for academic study. He was, in fact, the perfect person to launch an adult education platform in a format that would become known as "Community Colleges." Further, as the concept spread to the nation, Dr. Jaski was involved with further developments such as TV programming (that eventually evolved into the on-line availability of academic coursework), and developed an Executive Center (after retirement) to help place graduates into jobs. He further impacted a much wider community through **Impact, Inc.** (his company) and his work with the **Intl. Association of Educators for World Peace** that took him to several socialist countries to promote non-violent conflict resolution and facilitate communication within the international academic community.

Chicago Southtown Economist March 2003

Photos 2nd L toR: Dr. Jaski serving on advisory board for the Great Books Foundation; intl. educational travel
Photo(L): Tree planting 1985 for 25th yr of the founding of City Colleges of Chicago, first in the nation as a model college. Dr. Jaski recognized as Founding Faculty who implemented the Univ. of Chicago model for adult education.

Willdcats Northwestern Football　　　Dr. Ernest B. Jaski in China　　　Granddaughter Katherine (K.C.)

Jaster Golden Wedding Anniversary 2003

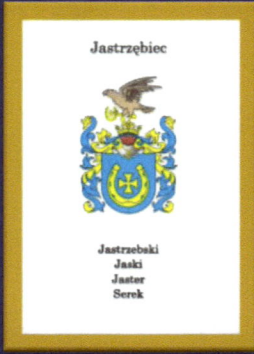

Jaster 50th Wedding Anniversary 2003

Present in photo (L to R): Marjorie Jaski, Tom Serek, John Patzelt, Gary Jaster, Julie & Len Jaster, Cindy Serek Patzelt, Leonard T. Jaster. Front: Albina Czapska Reinke and Florence Jaster.

In Loving Memory of
Leonard T. Jaster
April 24, 1924 - April 23, 2016

Leonard & Gary Jaster 2013

FLORENCE JASTER OBITUARY

Florence passed away in August 2019. Remembering Florence A. Jaster Salerno's Funeral Homes Florence A. Jaster Visitation Date: Friday, August 30, 2019 Visitation Time: 9:00-10:00 a.m. Funeral Home: Salerno's Rosedale Chapels Place of Funeral: Chapel Service at Salerno's Rosedale Chapels Interment: All Saints Cemetery Florence A. Jaster (nee Micus),age 93, of Bloomingdale, beloved wife of the late Leonard Jaster; devoted mother of Len (Julie) Jaster and Gary Jaster; loving daughter of the late Victor and Mary Micus; dear grandmother of Len (Cynthia) Jaster, Caitlin (Michael Manzo) Jaster, Mailee Jaster and the late Matthew Jaster; proud great grandmother of Ember Manzo and Brigit Jaster. 60172 (3/4 mile west of Bloomingdale/Roselle Rd.) Funeral Service will begin at 10:00 a.m. Interment All Saints Cemetery.

Photo left: Retired Commander Len Jaster with Officer Julie Jaster
Below: Esther's granddaughter Lisa, Tom Serek with son Tom and grandchildren.

Below: Leonard's younger son Gary with his daughter Mailee

Thomas Serek Obituary

Mr. Thomas "Trex" Anthony Serek, born on September 18, 1949, to the late Anthony and Esther(née Jastrzebski), passed away at age 69 on May 9, 2019 in Chicago, Illinois. He is survived by his daughter, Lisa(Brian)Berkery; son, Tom(Diana); sister, Cindy(John)Patzelt; and grandchildren, Nathan, Kassidy, Jake, Brooklyn, Jett, and Jack. Thomas was preceded in death by his dog, Seamus and leaves behind his adored dog, Mugwaum. Donations in Thomas' name to Orphans of the Storm are welcome and appreciated. Please call them at 847-945-0235 for more info.

Other Notable Achievements from Jastrzebski(s)

" Never doubt that a small group of thoughtful committed individuals can change the world. In fact, it's the only thing that ever has." -Margaret Mead

    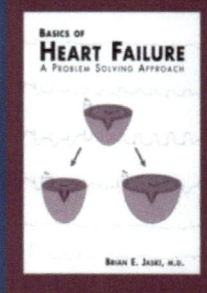

Since the High Middle Ages, Polish-sounding surnames ending with the masculine -*ski* suffix, including -*cki* and -*dzki*, and the corresponding feminine suffix -*ska/-cka/-dzka* were associated with the nobility (Polish *szlachta*), which alone, in the early years, had such suffix distinctions. They are widely popular today.

Jastrzębski (Polish pronunciation: [ja stsɛmpskii], feminine: **Jastrzębska**, plural: **Jastrzębscy**) is a Polish-language surname. It is a toponymic surname derived from one of the several Polish locations named Jastrzęby, Jastrzębie, Jastrząbki, etc. Ultimately derived from *jastrząb*, or "hawk".[1] Variants include Jastrzembski, Jastrząbski, and Yastrzemski. It is Russified as Yastrzhembsky/Yastrzhembskaya (Russian: Ястржембский).

Notable people with this surname include:

- Andrzej Jastrzębski (born 1939), Polish jazz tuba player
- Maria Jastrzębska (born 1953), Polish-British poet
- Stanisław Jastrzębski, Polish writer
- Włodzimierz Jastrzębski (born 1939), Polish historian and retired professor
- Józef Jastrzębski [pl] (1920-1989), Polish ethnographer
- Mirosława Jastrzębska (1921-1982), Polish ethnographer
- Nikolaus von Jastrzembski, birth name of Nikolaus von Falkenhorst (1885-1968), German
- Dennis Jastrzembski (born 2000), German footballer
- Steve Jastrzembski (1939–2009), American football player
- Sergey Yastrzhembsky (born 1953), Russian politician
- Carl Yastrzemski (born 1939), American baseball player
- Mike Yastrzemski (born 1990), American baseball player

Carl Yastrzemski: Folk Hero, Role Model, Icon
By Geoff Gehman

Wojciech Jastrzebski
Hackaday Prize 2023
For his revolutionary
3D printing technique

Yad Vashem Rescuer

Bogdan Jastrzebski receives Righteous Among the Nations award in 1989 as co-founder of Czech self-government.

Louis Jast, Founder 1931 National Library for the Blind

Champion Men's Volleyball since 1961

Polish American Society of Charleston Founded in 2011 by Gary Jaster

Poland as Member of NATO
Honoring the 25th Anniversary in 2024

SOURCE: WIKIMEDIA COMMONS

Polish Prime Minister Jerzy Buzek speaking October 15, 1998:

2025 Security first

As part of the celebration, Prime Minister Jerzy Buzek delivered Poland's first address to the North Atlantic Council as a NATO member, stating:

> "AFTER YEARS OF STRUGGLING FOR INDEPENDENCE AND SOVEREIGNTY, THE POLISH PEOPLE FORMALLY JOINED THE NORTH ATLANTIC COMMUNITY. LET ME ASSURE YOU THAT WE TAKE THE RESPONSIBILITY FOR THE SECURITY OF EACH INDIVIDUAL NATO MEMBER AND FOR THE INTERESTS OF THE ENTIRE ALLIANCE. UNDER THOSE FLAGS, WAVING IN THE WIND, ALLOW ME TO SAY: YOU CAN COUNT ON US. YOU CAN COUNT ON POLAND."

Appendix A: The Jastrzebski Clan Coat of Arms

The following was prepared from the classic heraldic reference Herbarz Polski *by Kasper Niesiecki, S J., Lipsk [Leipzig] edition, 1839-1846. The complete story may be found on the Polish Roots website listed below. Note, in older writings, the Clan Crest may also be called an "herb" and has nothing to do with cooking. -mj*

On a shield in a blue field is a gold horseshoe, with its heels pointed straight up, and in its center a cross; on the helmet over a crown is a Goshawk with its wings slightly raised for flight, facing the right side of the shield. On its legs are small bells and a leather strap, in its right talon it holds a horseshoe with cross, like those on the shield. Thus it is described by Paprocki *O herbach, f.,* 115; Okolski, vol. 1, fol. 315; Potocki, *Poczet herbów*, fol. 117; Bielski, fol. 83; Kojalowicz, in *MS*.

According to Paprocki, this armorial bearing has the name *Jastrzebiec* because the clan's ancestors, while still pagans, bore on the arms only a Goshawk (*Jastrzab*). But later, in the days of King Boleslaw the Brave, circa 999, when pagan foes were masters of Lysa Góra - two miles from Bozecin, now called Swiety Krzyz [Holy Cross] and stood secure upon it as if in a fortress, they hurled abuse upon our forces, saying: "Send forth one from among you who is willing to fight for Christ in a challenge against one of our men." Having heard this a knight, one Jastrzebczyk [scion of the Jastrzebiec clan], moved by the fervor of faith and the praise of God, invented shoes for the horses' hooves and, having shod a horse with them, succeeded in forcing his way up the mountain. He fought the Pagan, who had hitherto been jeering haughtily, captured him, and brought him to the King. After he had given the other soldiers of the Polish cavalry this method, when they had shod their horses and made their way up the slippery mountain, covered with ice, they destroyed and defeated the enemy.

As a reward for his ingenuity, he received from that King a variation of his arms, adding a horseshoe with a cross to the shield and elevating the Goshawk to the helmet. This is what Paprocki and all others who wrote about these arms say. I, however, cannot verify these authors' notion that this Jastrzebczyk in 999 was the first among us in Poland to invent the horseshoe and shoeing horses. For it is clear from antiquity that as early as Poppea (whose death in the days of Nero is described by Tacitus, *an. 16 Ulyss. Aldr. de quadrup. lib.* 1) she had her horse shod with silver shoes, and it is known that others before her used iron shoes, and I have mentioned vol 2, fol. 95 of *Balbin, Czech Historian*, that in Bohemia around the year 278 A.D. there was a house which used a seal with three horseshoes, and as he says, came with Czech to that country. And here in Poland, a foreign author also takes him to be the inventor of horseshoes. It is true, one might say, that our people did not use shoes for horses up to that time, and that Jastrzebczyk renewed this practice on the occasion already mentioned version. Nonetheless, as to the antiquity of this house, and the fact that it flourished even in pagan times in the Poland of the monarchs, all the authors agreed, and some add that one of the Jastrzebczyks was among the twelve voivodes who at two different times ruled the whole country.

The complete historical story may be found at:
www.polishroots.com/Research/Heraldry/HerbJastrzebiec?PageId=176

King Boleslaw (967-1025)
Poland's first king 1025/Piast Dynasty

What happened in 1000? It was called the Congress of Gniezno. The city was Poland's capital at that time, and during the congress the Emperor Otto III of the Holy Roman Empire, to which Poland was subordinate at that time, raised Gniezno to the rank of an archbishopric (which gave it a lot more meaning in the world political scene), and three new dioceses subordinate to Gniezno were created. Because of what he saw in Gniezno, and how powerful Poland appeared to be, and because the Emperor needed a strong ally, he placed his Imperial crown on Bolesław's brow and invested him with the title *frater et cooperator Imperii* ("Brother and Partner of the Empire"). Although it didn't give Bolesław much power, it was the beginning of his way towards the Crown of Poland.

The creation of the separate Archdiocese of Gniezno, as directly subordinate to the Holy See rather than a German archdiocese, kept Poland independent from the Holy Roman Empire throughout the Middle Ages. Around 1075 the Bishopric of Poznań became a suffragan diocese of Gniezno. The archdiocese then controlled the whole Piast realm, as confirmed by the papal Bull of Gniezno in 1136.

REFERENCE FOR KING BOLESLAW AND THE CONGRESS OF GNIEZNO:
https://en.wikipedia.org/wiki/Congress_of_Gniezno#:~:text=The%20creation%20of%20the%20separate,a%20suffragan%20diocese%2 0of%20Gnie; accessed 06/26/2025.

Appendix B: The Legend of Lech and the White Eagle

Three Brothers in Search of a New Home

Poland knows many variations of this legend, and it's one of the first Slavic stories that Polish children learn in their early years, included in majority of books with old Polish tales. Even though there are many small differences between the various versions, there's always the common plot that starts with the three brothers who departed together from their homeland in order to find a better place to live.

First to bid farewell was Rus, who chose to go eastward into the vast steppes where the wind was blowing freely.

Brother Czech left second with his tribe. He went westward, finding out about fertile lands (Czech version tells us that he settles in the area of the Říp Mountain located in the central Bohemian flatland).

Lech and his people kept going north, passing many uninhabited lands, but for a long time couldn't find anything that could feed them all. One day they stopped by exceptionally beautiful lands with thick forests and clean waters full of animals and fish, and decided to take a longer rest there.

Then, **they saw an unusual sight** which Lech and the tribe's elders interpreted as **a good omen**. A huge **white eagle** appeared on the sky and sat on a nearby oak where its nest was built. Before landing on the oak, the eagle stopped in the air with the wings wide open – its feathers were beautifully **contrasted with the red evening sky**.

After consultations with the elders, Lech decided to stay in that place. His tribe built there a fortress and named it **Gniezno** after a word meaning a 'nest'.

Excerpted story from https://slavorum.org/ancient-polish-legend-about-3-slavic-brothers-lech-czech-and-rus/; accessed 06/08/2025.
Artwork from European Amino Blog, *01/16/2022. Lech, Czech, and Rus the Founders of Three Slavic Nations.* <aminoapps.com/c/europeanamino/page/blog/lech-czech-and-rus-the-founders-of-three-slavic-nations/06Wa_qj1ckuYBKon0ER2Y3ve81EM0q3k8oX>; accessed 11/23/2024

Lech finds a white eagle and its nest. The Founding of Gniezno (Poland). Banner art by Michał Gorstkin-Wywiórski (1861-1926)

©ewka2205. *Sunset over the Baltic Sea* as published in *Polish Sunrise Sunset Times*. ©MAPLOGS.COM 2024, <https://sunrise.maplogs.com/poland.765.html>; accessed 12/16/2024. The lower red stripe of the Polish flag is emblematic of the red color of the evening sky as the sun sets over the Baltic Sea.

Distributed by
KDP
4900 Lacross Rd
North Charleston, SC 29406-6558

PRINTED IN THE UNITED STATES OF AMERICA

www.ingramcontent.com/pod-product-compliance
Lightning Source LLC
Chambersburg PA
CBHW042014150426
43196CB00002B/38